Guide to Massanutten Mountain Hiking Trails

Potomac Appalachian Trail Club

Vienna, VA

Text and diagrams by

Wil Kohlbrenner

Third Edition 2004

ISBN 0-915746-95-6

Library of Congress Control Number: 2003195214

Front cover: Catherine Furnace at Roaring Run Trail
Back cover: Mountain laurel, early June
(by Wil Kohlbrenner)

Contents

1. Introduction

THIS book provides complete information to guide hikers to all of the official Forest Service trails in the Massanutten Mountain section of the George Washington National Forest, Virginia. The Massanutten is a narrow range of parallel ridges approximately 50 miles in length. It runs roughly north-south, and separates the North and South Forks of the Shenandoah River. The mountain lies southeast of the intersection of Interstates 66 and 81.

The Massanutten's midpoint is crossed by US211 at New Market Gap, where the Forest Service maintains a Visitor Center. North of US211, the mountain ridges enclose a long valley, and the 71-mile long Massanutten Trail runs along the ridges surrounding that valley. South of US211, the 19-mile Massanutten South Trail runs the length of the southern section of the mountain. The guide describes some 50 additional trails and circuits.

Maps. References are given to PATC maps G and H, and Trails Illustrated map 792. These full-color, topographic maps show the terrain in the vicinity of the trails, as well as nearby towns and roads.

Mileage diagrams. Each group of trail descriptions has a mileage diagram to aid in planning hikes. The sketch shows only the mileage between trail intersections. Trails and roads are drawn as straight lines, which are *not* to scale and bear almost no relation to compass directions. Do not use the diagram as a substitute for a map.

Changes. Any guide is accurate only on its publication date. New trails may be constructed, old trails may be relocated or combined with others, blaze colors may be changed. Be prepared to adjust to situations that develop after publication.

This *Guide,* originally published in 1982 and updated in 2000, was extensively revised by Wil Kohlbrenner, a trail volunteer with the Forest Service and a PATC member.

Gaps and saddles. The Massanutten's ridges are long and narrow. A *gap* is a low point along a mountain ridge. The gap is part of the mountain ridge. The gap often has a name, for example, Edith Gap along the ridge of Massanutten Mountain.

Parallel ridges have a valley between them. A *saddle* is the highest point in the valley between two parallel ridges. The saddle has no name, and is not considered to be part of either mountain. The saddle, also called a *divide*, causes streams to flow in opposite directions, creating two *hollows* or *coves*, between the parallel ridges.

The near view. Popular overlooks, such as Signal Knob and Kennedy Peak, offer distant views, but haze often spoils the long view. Less-traveled trails offer near views at every step. Consider hiking for the flora and fauna. Or historical markers. Or geological formations. Or blueberries.

Glassy stones in an old roadbed may be slag from a furnace. Noisy crows may be harassing an owl. A passing shower may bring red efts onto the tread. A glass insulator hanging from a tree may have carried a phone line to a firetower. Yellow goatsbeard that you pass in the morning may be closed by afternoon. A doe that runs off flashing her white tail may be distracting you from her fawn hidden in the brush.

There are mysteries to be solved. How did this sassafras tree get broken? What animal left this ropey scat on the rock? And why? How did this big flat rock get moved to the middle of this grassy roadbed? Is this rock ledge older than the ledge in the valley? Did the yellow jackets dig that hole in the ground? Why did that black snake climb into the laurel? Are there fossils in these rocks? What is this shrub that has fruit and flowers at the same time? What are those fuzzy orange spots on trees?

Forest Service. The forest is administered by the United States Forest Service, an arm of the Department of Agriculture. The Forest Service was formed in the early 1900s with a charter to preserve watersheds and wisely manage the nation's dwindling forests.

The public land on the Massanutten was purchased over many years. Expansion has ceased, although private parcels that are surrounded by public land are occasionally purchased. This is the George Washington National Forest. It is administratively combined with the Jefferson National Forest and is often referred to as the George Washington and Jefferson National Forests. The forest is divided into districts, and Massanutten lies within the northernmost district, the Lee Ranger District.

Trails. Many of the trails on the Massanutten were made centuries ago by the wagons of settlers, tanbark gatherers, iron miners, and charcoal makers. These old roads are visible now only as faint disturbances of the forest floor, but some remain in use as trails. Some trails are kept open as 4WD roads (usually behind a locked gate), which increases the trail's usefulness in emergencies. The annual growth of brush threatens to close off most trails each year. Forest Service personnel and volunteers are hard-pressed to cut all this brush, so the Forest Service may spray selected trails with an herbicide to retard growth.

Blazing standards. Two blazing standards are used to mark trails on the Massanutten, the Lee District standard and the Tuscarora Trail standard.

The Lee District standard is a "dotted-i" blaze—a square "dot" above a vertical rectangle. The dotted-i blaze is a replacement for the earlier practice of marking trails with an axe – early trail blazers left "a hack and a slash" on trees along the trail. The hack became the dot and the slash became the rectangle. Some trails have a V-shaped blaze. V-blazed trails are open to motorized vehicles, specifically motorcycles, all-terrain vehicles (ATVs), and off-highway (4WD or OHV) vehicles.

Six colors are used: pink, orange, yellow, blue, purple, and white. When two trails run concurrently on the same tread, the blazes of both appear, sometimes on the same tree.

The Tuscarora Trail standard is identical to the Appalachian Trail standard, but uses blue paint instead of white. The blaze is a vertical rectangle, without a "dot." In order to provide a consistent blaze for backpackers on the Tuscarora, the Lee District permits the use of this simple blue rectangle. The Tuscarora blaze standard also specifies the stacking of two rectangles to indicate an obscure turn in the trail, with the upper blaze offset in the direction of the turn.

Other colors: red paint is reserved for the marking of trees along the boundary of the forest, to separate National Forest land from privately owned land. Silver "blazes" along the boundaries of private property may be painted by the property owner to indicate "no hunting."

Unblazed trails that are on private property or lead off public land onto private property are not described in this guide.

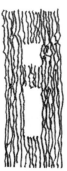

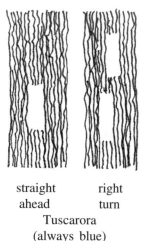

dotted-i blaze
Lee District
(white, blue, pink,
purple, yellow, orange)

straight   right
ahead   turn
Tuscarora
(always blue)

Trail signs. The Forest Service uses a yearly sign budget to erect new signs at trailheads and trail intersections, but vandalism seems to keep pace with new signs. Rely on blaze color to identify the trail.

Motorized trails. About 35 miles of trails are open to motorized vehicles, such as Off-Highway Vehicles (4x4), motorized trail bikes, and All-Terrain Vehicles (ATV). They are open to all trail users, but are generally avoided by hikers and are not described in this guide. If you hike on them, expect dust clouds in dry weather, slick surfaces and flying mud in wet weather, trash, and nonforest noise. These trails are busy on weekends.

Going off-trail. Bushwhacking, orienteering, and explorations off a blazed trail are permitted. Note that there are private land holdings that are entirely surrounded by national forest. Use a map that shows these inholdings so that you can stay off of private property. Also, see *Hunting*, under *Trail Hazards*.

Multi-use. All of the Lee District's blazed trails are open to hikers, horse and mule riders, and mountain bike riders. Be prepared to share the trail with these users. A horse may feel threatened by a hiker with a towering backpack, hiking poles, or a brightly colored poncho. A *friendly conversation* with the rider often calms the horse and rider. Bikers are required to yield to hikers and equestrians, but a biker struggling to pedal up a steep, narrow ascent will appreciate the hiker who steps off the trail.

Most dotted-i trails are closed to all motorized vehicles, and you are urged to report any misuse by motorcycles or all-terrain vehicles to the Lee District headquarters (540-984-4101). If you can obtain a license plate number from the rider's vehicle near the trailhead, the Forest Service will follow up.

Forest roads. Dirt roads are constructed to develop areas for logging. Unlike national park lands, a national forest is managed for long-term productivity of its forest products. When a logging operation is over, the road provides a ribbon of edge habitat through the forest. Roads are useful in fighting fires, since they form a ready-made fire break, and make it easy to transport personnel, equipment, and water to where it is needed.

A forest road's number may appear on a map. Most roads have a STOP sign where the road emerges, and the road's number is usually painted on the post.

Gates. Most forest roads have a locked gate to limit vehicle traffic. Foot, mountain bike, and horse traffic is permitted on a forest road, even when its gate is closed. Some gates are open year-round, but may be locked temporarily when melting snow or heavy rains soften the road surface. A gate that is closed year-round may be opened for a month to allow the gathering of fuel-wood (downed trees), since the periodic removal of dead wood reduces the fuel available to a wildfire. A fuel wood permit is required.

Skid trails. During logging, trees are cut into appropriate lengths and then "skidded" to a log landing, where they are loaded onto trucks that transport them to sawmills. The skidder leaves a wide path of disturbed earth. When the logging operation is over, these skid trails are shaped with earth-moving equipment to control runoff. The bare earth is seeded with species of grass that will reduce erosion and be of benefit to wildlife. Skid trails are allowed to grow back into forest.

Clearings. Most clearings on the Massanutten were constructed after a logging operation, when certain areas of the clearcut were seeded with desirable species of ground cover. For example, log landings are often left as clearings. Clearings increase the diversity of wildlife by providing more edge habitat for creatures that move between the clearing and nearby woods. Clearings are used in fighting forest fires as staging areas for water and equipment; some can even be used by helicopters. Each clearing requires mowing every few years to keep it from reverting to forest.

Ponds. All the ponds on the Massanutten were constructed, often after a logging operation, in an area where there is a natural spring or seep. The ponds are created to increase the diversity of wildlife, and to provide a water source for wildlife during times of drought. They are also a ready source of water in the event of a forest fire.

Streams. Water in most streams is too acidic (from acid rain) to support the delicate food chain required for fish reproduction. Finely ground limestone is dumped at some stream edges to correct the pH level. *Be sure to purify any water prior to drinking.*

Prescribed burns. The Forest Service occasionally sets a selected area of the forest on fire. Carefully controlled operations, Prescribed burns occur only after a period of warnings to adjacent landowners and surrounding communities. Firebreaks are prepared, and the fire is started only when weather predictions and various measurements of moisture at the ground level point to the desired result. Usually, the intent is to burn off the low vegetation and dead wood on the ground, while sparing most of the standing trees and the forest duff. This opens the woods beneath the canopy, making it less likely to support an unwanted fire and more hospitable to certain wildlife, such as grouse and wild turkey.

Passage Creek Day Use Area. The forest land at the north end of Fort Valley sees a high concentration of visitors, for camping, hiking, fishing, and picnicking. Camping in this area is restricted to the designated campgrounds.

Dogs. Your pet is welcome in the forest, but be sure to read *Dog Safety* under *Trail Hazards.*

Fishing and hunting. State regulations apply. State licenses and a National Forest stamp are required. See separate discussion of hunting under *Trail Hazards.*

Camping terminology. The trail descriptions in this guide use the terms shelter, tentsite, campsite, potential tentsite, and hunter campsite.

Shelter. This is a roofed, three-sided wooden structure with fire ring, privy and water source nearby. There are two on the Massanutten: Little Crease Shelter on the Massanutten Tr and Boone Run Shelter on the Massanutten South Tr. They may be used by hunters. *Hazard trees are removed every winter.*

Tentsite. This is a smooth, almost-level area at least 7 by 9 feet. *Hazard trees may be present.*

Campsite. This is a fire ring combined with one or more tentsites (*multi-tent* means three or more tentsites). These are hardened sites, used mostly by hikers, seldom by hunters. *Hazard trees may be present.*

 **Tent icons.** When a tentsite or campsite cannot be seen from the trail, there is usually an unblazed path leading to it. To distinguish such a path from paths to overlooks and paths made by hunters and animals, tent icons are painted on trees facing the trail user. The tent icon is a white tepee shape. A tent icon is signaled in the trail's description by △.

Potential tentsite. (Leave-No-Trace area) This is an area of almost level ground, under deep canopy, that has no plant growth – only leaf litter, where it is possible to camp without leaving evidence that *anyone* has *ever* camped there. *Hazard trees may be present.* See *Leave-no-Trace Camping,* below.

Hunter campsite. This is a pull-off area along an open forest road, with a fire ring. Some have a tentsite, but most users sleep in a camper. Hunter campsites are jammed with hunters during the two-week general firearm season for deer, but otherwise they are lightly used and are not reserved for hunters. (The Forest Service calls this a dispersed vehicle campsite.) *Hazard trees may be present.*

Forest Service developed campgrounds. These offer a pull-off for your vehicle, a level tent pad, picnic table, grill, fire ring, pole for a lantern, a nearby tested water source, restrooms. There are three: Elizabeth Furnace, Camp Roosevelt, and Little Fort. Three large-group campsites at Elizabeth Furnace must be reserved in advance, but all other family-sized sites are available on a first-come, first-served basis. Check with the Forest Service for dates of operation and facilities available. *Hazard trees are removed every winter.*

Reliability of water sources. All water sources are described as *reliable* or *unreliable*. Reliable means you are likely to find water during a drought; unreliable means the source may dry up after only a few weeks of dry weather. During a drought, water in a reliable stream may be moving underground, but you can usually find water in pools along the streambed.

Caution: "reliable" does not mean that the water is safe to drink without treatment. All water should be treated before drinking it or using it to wash utensils. You should carefully study the location of water sources and campsites to estimate how much water to carry on each section of the trail.

Caching water. The word "cache" indicates a location where you might consider hiding a plastic jug of water before beginning a backpacking trip.

A water cache can be left near a road crossing or near the intersection of a side trail. Walk along the trail far from the intersect point until you find a prominent feature that you will be able to recognize again (examples: rock outcrop, uprooted tree, multiple-trunk tree). Hide the water jug nearby, but well off the trail, perhaps dug into the leaf mold behind a log or rock. Cover it with leaf litter. Count steps back to the trail, then back to the intersection, and *write it all down.*

Do not use flagging tape to indicate a cache point. Flagging tape gets removed, and items hidden near flagging have been removed.

Some cached water jugs have been punctured, probably by animals. If you are driving around eating your lunch and you then handle a jug with a food smell still on your hands, forest scavengers (bear, skunk, raccoon, possum) will be attracted by the food odor and bite the jug. Remove food odors from your hands, then rub leaves and duff between your hands. Be sure to hide the jug from human eyes under leaves and small brush. Avoid hanging the jug in a tree, especially during hunting season.

Campfires. Use campstoves for cooking. If you make a campfire in an existing fire ring, clear leaves and twigs away from the ring. Use only small breakable twigs, or cut small dead branches with a handsaw. Use wood pieces that will be completely burned up before the need to extinguish the fire. Never place a long branch or log across the fire ring.

A fire permit is not required. Between February 15th and April 30th, Virginia law allows such a fire only between the hours of 4 p.m. and midnight. *A campfire must be attended at all times.* You cannot attend a campfire while asleep in your tent, so campfires must be dead out before retiring for the night. Before lighting a fire, insure that you have sufficient water to extinguish it. Mix water with the coals and stir into the mineral dirt. Feel the dirt with your bare hands to be sure the fire is out. A fire is not "smothered" by throwing dirt on it, or rolling rocks into the ring.

Usually, the Forest Service bans campfires only if Virginia has declared a ban on open fires. The open-fire ban is enforced with stiff fines. However, a ban on open fires usually does not include backpacker stoves. Check with the Forest Service before a camping trip to learn of fire bans and drought conditions.

Trash. Carry out all trash. Do not bury it or try to burn it. A plastic water jug can be flattened and hung from your pack. (A plastic jug that is flattened and left under leaf litter may trap rain water and be a breeding place for mosquitoes.) Trash can be left in bins at some picnic areas, as noted in the trail descriptions.

Body waste. Whether camping or just day-hiking, dig a "cat-hole" at least 200 feet from any water source, and cover body waste and toilet paper with six inches of soil. Urine need not be buried.

Leave-No-Trace camping. Hikers who go off-trail to find their own campsite should practice leave-no-trace camping. *Do not* create a new campsite by clearing brush, leveling the ground, building a fire ring. Instead, choose a level, smooth site that is covered only with leaves or pine needles. Cook on a portable stove. Use a candle lantern for light. If you must have a campfire, you should use an existing campsite.

Trail hazards. *The Potomac Appalachian Trail Club expressly denies any liability for any accident or injury to persons or their pets when using these trails. Hikers should be aware of various hazards on the trails.*

Your welfare in the National Forest is your responsibility. You must exercise common sense before starting out. Even a short hike to a lookout requires that you wear sturdy footgear, know the weather forecast, dress appropriately, and carry food and water. You must leave sufficient time to return to your vehicle.

If you hike alone, leave your itinerary and a description of your vehicle with a friend, and a time when you expect to check in with that friend. Then stick to your plan!

If you become incapacitated on a trail, become lost, or if night comes while you are still on the trail, you may experience a long delay in receiving aid. *Cellular phones do not work from most trail locations.* A rescue helicopter will not be able to land on a wooded trail, or a rocky ridge. Resources and personnel will have to be gathered to effect your rescue. Rescue personnel may have to hike a long distance, then carry you out along a narrow, steep, rocky trail. *You may spend a night on the mountain.*

Your inattention to trail hazards, hiking conditions, and remaining daylight hours can jeopardize your survival.

Dehydration is the most significant hazard, usually striking casual hikers who overestimate their ability to deal with steep trails and underestimate the need to drink water. In winter, most fluid loss is through your breath; in summer through sweating. Dehydration leads to headache and dizziness, leg cramps, and weakness. The risk of a dangerous fall increases, often near the end of the day when you are hiking down a steep, rocky trail. Each hiker should begin the hike with at least two quarts of water. Drink water before you feel thirsty, since thirst is a sign that you are already dehydrated.

Hunting occurs in the National Forest from October to May. Hunting schedules are published yearly by the Virginia Department of Game and Inland Fisheries. A free booklet is available through the Forest Service and at most sporting goods stores. All trails described in this guide are in the Virginia counties of Shenandoah, Page, Warren, and Rockingham.

Hikers should stay out of the National Forest when deer are hunted with modern firearms, usually a two- or three-week period in late November and early December. Note that some hunters may shoot at trail blazes – wearing blaze orange may not protect you from this danger.

During the rest of hunting season, hikers should wear blaze orange clothing, and avoid white, brown, and black colors. Remain on blazed trails and make noise as you hike.

Under current regulations in Virginia, there is no hunting on Sundays.

Two venomous snakes, the timber rattlesnake and the copperhead, live throughout this area. These snakes may inject a hemotoxic venom if they strike you. The venom is slow-acting if it is not injected directly into a vein. If bitten, remain calm, but *immediately* seek medical care at a hospital in Front Royal, Woodstock, or Harrisonburg. (Please do not kill any snakes – they are part of the ecology of the mountain.)

Black bears live throughout this area. Bears are hunted every fall, so they are wary of humans. A bear will move away from the scent or sound of a human coming along the trail. The primary danger occurs when you come *silently* around a turn in the trail and find yourself near a sow and her cubs. A dog, even on a leash, may further provoke the bear. Make noise as you move along the trail to avoid this situation. If you backpack, observe the usual precaution of hanging all food (including dogfood and scented items) between trees well away from your tent site, to avoid bears, as well as skunks, raccoons, etc.

Coyotes. Coyotes are on the increase. They pose no problem for humans, but dogs are at risk. See *Dog Safety*, below.

Other animals, such as raccoon, fox, bobcat, opossum, skunks, and feral housecats live in the forest. They are rarely seen, and pose no threat to humans or dogs – unless the wild animal is sick or injured. Keep away from an animal that is not fleeing from you.

Yellow jackets, small yellow-and-black striped wasps that live in abandoned rodent holes, are a significant threat. If you step on or close to the nest hole, the threatened wasps will attack in numbers. Each wasp can deliver *multiple* stings (unlike bees). These are painful, but the danger is that body tissues may swell from a reaction to the wasp venom and shut down your ability to breathe. You are unlikely to encounter a wasp nest if you stay on the trail, but exploring off the trail, looking for firewood near camp, berry picking, or "using the woods" puts you at risk.

Falling trees. Many trees that were killed in recent decades by gypsy moth defoliation are still standing, minus smaller limbs and bark. As the roots rot away, these snags resemble tall, one-ton bowling pins stood on end. The tree may fall at any time. Choose a campsite well away from these snags. Some campers write "LOOK UP" on their tent bag as a reminder.

Dog safety. In campgrounds and picnic areas, a dog must be kept on a leash. On a trail, the leash is not required. However, a dog that is running loose is at risk. A bear that is chased by a dog may turn and kill the dog. A rattlesnake will strike a barking dog on the nose or forepaws. A sick skunk can still spray. A fox with distemper or rabies can still bite. Yellow jackets will sting a nose that is poked into their nest (and ears, eyes, lips). A hunter may shoot the dog. Coyotes can easily kill a small dog. Attempting to rescue your dog from these hazards also endangers you.

Also, if your dog ranges ahead and barks at what it finds, it may startle an equestrian or mountain biker and cause a fall.

Dehydration strikes dogs as well as humans. Be sure to give your dog water at every rest stop. A dog that is accustomed to grassy fields and smooth floors at home may not have paws that are tough enough for a rocky trail. During hunting season, put blaze orange on the dog as well as yourself. When camping, keep the dog in your tent at night, but be sure to hang its food with your food, well away from the tent.

If your dog becomes incapacitated on a trail, you will have to evacuate the dog yourself. Rescue squads and county police and fire departments cannot commit their resources to the rescue of injured animals.

Hiking difficulty. Each trail description supplies information to aid in gauging hiking difficulty. The following terms are used.

Mileage. This is given to the nearest tenth of a mile. Mileage on trail signs may be rounded to the nearest mile and is likely to differ from the mileage in this guide.

Rise. This is the difference between the lowest and highest elevations on the trail.

Elevation. Elevation in feet is supplied at low and high points, enclosed in square brackets. These numbers are estimated from USGS maps and are rounded to the nearest ten feet.

Block field. The trail crosses an area of large tipped rocks, with no flat, dirt areas between the rocks.

Gutted. The trail's surface has eroded, exposing large rocks and roots.

Loose tread. The trail's surface has many loose rocks that shift underfoot.

Steep. The grade often exceeds 20% (20 feet of elevation gain for every 100 feet of horizontal travel).

Hidden hazards. Large loose rocks, slanted roots, or slippery mud may be hidden in lush grass or under leaves.

Mudhole. A pool of standing water and thick mud.

Scramble. Very steep tread, usually on tipped or unevenly spaced rocks. Coming down may be harder than going up.

No blazed trail requires mountain climbing gear.

Potomac Appalachian Trail Club (PATC)

Founded in 1927, the PATC is one of 32 organizations maintaining the Appalachian Trail under the Appalachian Trail Conference, and is the third largest club in number of members. Volunteer-driven, PATC maintains trails in Virginia, Maryland, and Southern Pennsylvania, including trails in the George Washington National Forest, Shenandoah National Park, and other regional parks. The club also developed a 251-mile side trail to the Appalachian Trail (*AT*) known as the Tuscarora Trail running from the *AT* in SNP through Hancock, MD, and reconnecting with the *AT* north of Carlisle, PA. PATC also maintains a network of shelters and cabins, and publishes maps, guidebooks, and general interest books.

The club has an active Mountaineering Section, which offers assistance and training in rock climbing techniques as well as more difficult climbing opportunities for the advanced climber. A Ski Touring Section conducts workshops for beginners, participates in work trips to improve ski trails in local areas, and organizes ski trips to local and distant ski areas.

PATC's Trail Patrol makes regular patrols within PATC's trail region, assisting hikers and providing information on trail routes and conditions. It also offers training for backpackers. The Shenandoah Mountain Rescue Group is a semi-professional group of volunteers dedicated to wilderness search and rescue and outdoor safety education.

A call to PATC or visit to the club's website will provide information on trail, shelter, and cabin work trips, as well as other activities conducted by the club. A recorded message outlining trips and activities for the upcoming week can be heard at 703-242-0965. The club's website, www.patc.net, has a wealth of information and resources, including secure on-line ordering of maps and publications, information about PATC cabin rentals, and an interactive Trails Forum for discussion of the outdoors.

2. Road Approaches

ALL roads are numbered, and usually are named. Since name signs are occasionally stolen, it is better to rely on the number.

In the descriptions, road numbers begin with a letter code. Interstate highways begin with I, federal highways with US, secondary roads with SR, forest roads with FR. A forest road's number is usually painted as yellow digits on the post that holds a stop sign where the forest road meets another road.

Mileage. Mileage was taken from an automobile odometer.

Direction. Most road approaches are described as either a north-south route or an east-west route. These are approximate headings. Mileage is supplied for travel in either direction. Turns to the right or left of the direction of travel are given as compass headings that are at right angles to the line of travel. Thus, along a north-south road approach, most turns are indicated using the words "west" and "east" rather than "left" and "right." This makes most road approaches readable in both directions. Since these headings are approximate, actual compass readings will be of no use and may be misleading.

Road surfaces. Forest and secondary roads are often gravel-surfaced. Gravel provides poor traction, especially on curves.

Parking. A number in parenthesis indicates the approximate number of spaces in a parking area. When parking at a trailhead, or a road that leads to a trailhead, do not block trail access for emergency vehicles.

Winter conditions. Forest roads are not plowed in winter.

U. S. Highway
Luray – New Market (US211)
This major highway connects the towns of Luray and New Market, by crossing the Massanutten Mountain between its north and south halves, in New Market Gap.

West   East

0.0   14.0   Center of Luray. Junction of US211 BUSINESS, Main Street, and US340 BUSINESS, Broad Street. Take US211 west. If entering Luray from Front Royal on US340, avoid the center of Luray by turning right, west, onto US211-US340 BYPASS. US211's BUSINESS and BYPASS routes merge west of Luray.

1.3   12.7   Junction of US211 BUSINESS and US211 BYPASS.

5.3   8.7   SR615 crosses. Stay on US211. (A turn to the north onto SR615 leads to SR675 and SR684 in 5.7 miles, see separate road approach, Edinburg – Luray, below.)

6.6   7.4   SR615 rejoins from south. Ignore this, continue on US211.

7.3   6.7   US340 BYPASS turns south, leading to Newport and the north end of Cub Run Rd, see separate road approach, Cub Run Rd, below. Stay on US211. Westbound, the highway narrows to three lanes, two ascending to the west and one descending to the east. Eastbound, road becomes dual highway.

8.1   5.9   Massanutten South Tr, orange-blazed, south. Massanutten Connector Tr, white-blazed, north. Parking (20), south. Westbound traffic must turn left from the passing lane! If traffic is heavy, drive to the top of the mountain, turn around in the Visitor Center, and descend to this point.

10.2   3.8   New Market Gap. Forest Service Visitor Center, south. Westbound traffic *has the center lane reserved* for turning.

10.3   3.7   FR274, Crisman Hollow Rd, north. See separate road approach, Crisman Hollow Rd. Eastbound traffic *has the center lane reserved* for turning.

12.6   1.4   Cross Shenandoah North Fork. Eastbound, road narrows to three lanes, two ascending, one descending.

14.0   0.0   New Market. Junction of US211 with US11 at a traffic light. To access I-81, turn south on US11 and follow signs through center of New Market. Eastbound drivers coming from I-81 must go east to the center of New Market, then north on US11 to this traffic light.

Secondary Roads

Fort Valley Rd (SR678)

This secondary road is the central route in this picturesque valley enclosed within the Massanutten's north half. The road has two narrow, paved lanes, narrow shoulders, and many bends and dips with poor sight lines, but it is usually traveled at 50 mph by locals. Try pulling off onto side roads to admire the scenery.

South	North	
0.0	**20.2**	Waterlick. On VA55, 5 mi west of US 340-522 in Front Royal, and 5 mi east of US11 in Strasburg.

1.2   19.0   SR619 east, leads to Bentonville. See separate road approach, Waterlick – Bentonville.

3.4   16.8   Signal Knob Parking and Massanutten Tr access at nominal start point for CCW and CW trail descriptions. Parking lot (40) west.

3.6   16.6   Elizabeth Furnace Group Campground, east. Reservation required at Forest Service office in Edinburg, VA. (The Group Campground is usually reserved months in advance.)

4.0   16.2   Elizabeth Furnace Picnic Area, east, with access to Massanutten Tr (west CCW 70.3, east CW 0.8). There are two parking areas. Outer parking (10) before the bridge over Passage Creek is always open. A gate on the far side of the bridge is closed and locked every evening. Note the gate closing time before driving through it to inner parking (30).

4.3   15.9   A pull-off (1), east to access the Elizabeth Furnace Log Cabin. More parking at the Family Campground.

4.4   15.8   Elizabeth Furnace Family Campground, east. Overnight use, no reservations. Mudhole Gap Tr, purple-blazed, begins on a forest road that goes west directly opposite the campground entrance. Parking (10) in various places along this forest road before a locked gate. Hunter campsites on a loop road to the south of the forest road before the gate.

5.0 15.2 Sherman Gap Tr, pink-blazed, crosses road. Parking (40), west. Very busy place when an equestrian event is being held.

5.9 14.3 Glass House driveway, west, at "GLASS" mailbox. The steep driveway is locked, and a reservation is needed from the Potomac Appalachian Trail Club. If you are driving south, this is a very sharp right turn – it may be better to drive past it, continue south until you have a chance to turn around, then drive north for an easy left turn into the driveway.

8.7 11.5 SR771, Boyer Rd, west. Leads to FR273 and FR66. See separate road approach, Powells Fort Camp, below.

10.4 9.8 SR774, east. Leads to Veach Gap Tr parking (8) in 1.0 mi.

12.0 8.2 SR758 to east. Ignore this; it loops to Detrick.

12.9 7.3 Detrick. SR758 crosses. See separate road approach, Detrick – Woodstock, below.

20.2 0.0 Kings Crossing. SR675 crosses. See separate road approach, Edinburg – Luray, below.

Edinburg – Luray (SR675)

This numbered secondary road connects the town of Edinburg, on the Shenandoah North Fork, with Kings Crossing near the south end of Fort Valley. It then rises through Edith Gap, and continues east across the Shenandoah South Fork to Luray. This is the main east-west route across the northern half of Massanutten Mountain. The road has many different names, but the route number is constant across both Shenandoah and Page Counties.

East West

0.0 17.9 Edinburg. Junction of SR675 with US11, 0.5 mi north of the center of Edinburg, bisecting an auto dealership. Drive east on SR675, called Fort St. Westbound traffic, turn left and stay on SR675 through Edinburg to access I-81.

0.1 17.8 Edinburg town limit. Eastbound, the road becomes Edinburg Gap Rd.

4.0 13.9 Edinburg Gap. Parking (10), south. Massanutten Tr (south CCW 22.4, north CW 48.7), orange-blazed, crosses. OHV and ATV trails, V-blazed, also cross road. FR374, south, see separate road approach, Edinburg Gap Forest Rd, below.

4.5 **13.4** Popular piped spring, north, in a pull-off.

4.8 **13.1** Taskers Gap Tr, OHV, south, gated forest road.

5.9 **12.0** Kings Crossing. SR678 crosses. To go north, see separate road approach, Fort Valley Rd. Eastbound, turn right, then bear left at fork, SR675 is then called Camp Roosevelt Rd. Westbound, turn left on SR675, now called Edinburg Gap Rd.

7.9 **10.0** Ignore SR678, west, which loops to Kings Crossing.

9.3 **8.6** Junction with SR730 to west, and FR274 to south. See separate road approaches for Moreland Gap Rd (SR730) and Crisman Hollow Rd (FR274), below. Eastbound, bear left around curve. Westbound, bear right around curve. CAUTION: This is a dangerous intersection since the through traffic on SR675 is rounding a blind curve.

9.6 **8.3** Camp Roosevelt Recreation Area, north. Camping and picnicking, no reservations. The first Civilian Conservation Corps camp, NF-1, was built here in the 1930s.

9.7 **8.2** Massanutten Tr (north CCW 46.1, south CW 25.0), orange-blazed, crosses. The trail north of SR675 uses the entrance road to a large parking lot (15). Also, parking along SR675 for a few vehicles.

11.0 **6.9** Edith Gap, on ridge of Massanutten Mountain. Massanutten Tr (north on ridge CCW 47.0, west into Fort Valley CW 24.1), orange-blazed, joins the road, for 35 yds. Parking (15) both sides of road.

13.9 **4.0** Eastbound, a T-junction, turn left, now called Egypt Bend Rd. Westbound, turn right, now called Camp Roosevelt Rd. (Egypt Bend Rd goes south from here as SR615, to US211-US340 in 5.7 miles.)

14.4 **3.5** Bixlers Ferry Bridge. Eastbound, bear right onto bridge, now called Bixler Ferry Rd. Westbound, bear left at fork, now called Egypt Bend Rd. (SR684, Page Valley Rd, starts north here – see separate road approach, Page Valley Rd, below)

17.8   0.1   Luray town limit. Eastbound, road is called Mechanic St, westbound road is called Bixler Ferry Rd.

17.9   0.0   Luray. Junction of SR675, Mechanic St, with US340 BUSINESS, North Broad Street. The center of Luray is 0.1 mi south on US340 BUSINESS. Ramps to US211/US340 BYPASS are 0.5 mi north, see separate road approach, Luray – New Market, above.

   NOTE: To drive westbound on SR675 you must be on US340 BUSINESS. There is no exit directly onto SR675 from the US340 BYPASS. If you are entering Luray on US211 from the east, take the US211 BYPASS, but be sure to exit at signs for US340 BUSINESS and then turn left at the end of the ramp to find the Mechanic St intersection.

Detrick – Woodstock (SR758, SR665)

These secondary roads connect Detrick, near the center of Fort Valley, with Woodstock, the county seat. Despite the very narrow switchbacks on the west of the mountain, this is a commuting route for people who live in Fort Valley and is used by commercial vehicles.

West   East

0.0   8.5   Detrick, on SR678, Fort Valley Rd. See separate road approach, Fort Valley Rd. Drive west on SR758, Woodstock Tower Rd, paved, steep ascent at the turn.

1.6   6.9   Road surface change: paved east, gravel west.

2.7   5.8   Little Fort Recreation Area entrance, south.

3.2   5.3   Peters Mill Run Tr (OHV), yellow-V-blazed, south. Parking area along the trail.

3.3   5.2   Sharp turn in SR758. FR273 goes north here, see separate road approach, Powells Fort Camp. Gate on SR758 above the turn may be locked if the road surface is unsafe due to storms.

4.0   4.5   Gap between Powell and Three Top mountains. Woodstock Tower Tr, pink-blazed, south. Parking (8) both sides of road. Begin descent, either direction.

4.1   4.4   Massanutten Tr (south CCW 14.2, north CW 56.9), orange-blazed, crosses. Parking (30), both sides of the road. Westbound, continue descent.

The road is gravel-surfaced and often only one lane wide with pull-outs to allow oncoming traffic to pass. There are many sharp switchbacks, but the turns are paved.

6.1   2.4   Forest boundary. Gate here may be locked if road surface is unsafe due to storms. Eastbound, ascend. Westbound, road is wider and paved.

6.5   2.0   Burnshire bridge, with dam upstream.

7.1   1.4   Junction of SR758, Woodstock Tower Rd, with SR665, Mill Rd. Westbound, turn right onto SR665. Eastbound, bear left onto SR758.

8.5   0.0   Woodstock. Junction of SR665, Mill Rd, with US11 at north end of a shopping center at north end of town. To reach I-81 southbound, turn south on US11, go 2 mi through Woodstock and follow signs. For I-81 northbound, turn right on US-11, go 6 mi through Toms Brook to Mount Olive Rd, follow signs.

Moreland Gap Rd (SR730)

This county road connects the south end of Fort Valley with a point on US11 between Mt. Jackson and New Market. Moreland Gap lies between Bowman and Kerns Mountains. On both sides of the gap, the road uses low-water bridges to cross creeks that drain east and west. Both ends of the road are paved, but the center section is gravel-surfaced, and in a few places only one lane wide. There are some hunter campsites, but be sure you are in the national forest, not on private property.

East   West

0.0   8.8   Junction of US11 and SR730, Moreland Gap Rd. This is 2.3 mi south of Mt. Jackson and 4.6 mi north of New Market. Flat farmland, known as Meems Bottom. Eastbound, take SR730, paved.

0.7   8.1   Bridge over Smith Creek.

1.2   7.6   Sharp turn, surface change: paved west, gravel east.

5.4   3.4   High point of road – a large, open intersection. FR374 north, see separate road approach, Edinburg Gap Forest Rd, below. Parking here (5) for Massanutten Tr.

5.5   3.3   Massanutten Tr (south CCW 30.4, north CW 40.7), orange-blazed, crosses.

7.5   1.3   Taskers Gap Tr, north. Hard to find. Parking (5) along the road well *east* of this point. (Taskers Gap Tr is not described in this guide, because it becomes an ATV-OHV road and leads into a complex of ATV trails.)

8.1   0.7   Surface change: gravel west, paved east.

8.8   0.0   Junction of SR730, Moreland Gap Rd, with SR675, Camp Roosevelt Rd, and FR274, Crisman Hollow Rd. See separate road approaches, Edinburg – Luray, above, and Crisman Hollow Rd, below.

Page Valley Rd (SR684, SR717)

These two numbered roads with one name run along the Shenandoah South Fork, between the river and the Massanutten Mountain, as a dead-end road. The road crosses fingers of national forest land that extend down the slope of the mountain to the river.

Mailbox numbers for private houses along the road provide a mileage measure, e.g., box 2345 marks the 2.3 mile point, but the mailboxes become scarce as you drive north.

North

0.0   West end of Bixlers Ferry Bridge on SR675. See separate road approach, Edinburg – Luray, above. Drive north on SR684, paved.

6.0   Bealers Ferry, right. Canoe launching area.

6.8   Road surface change: north gravel, south paved.

7.5   Foster's Landing, right. The sign says only, "Public Boat Landing." Parking here (15) for Habron Gap Tr. The trailhead is just north of the entrance to the parking area.

8.5   Turn left onto SR717. (SR684 continues to a dead-end.)

9.9   Pasture between road and river.

10.9   Pasture ends as road rises, away from river.

11.5   Indian Grave Ridge Tr. (Turn left at the high point of the road to reach a parking area (8) and the trailhead.) Continue north, descending.

12.8   Pasture between road and river, called Burners Bottom.

13.1   Public boat launch area, restrooms, on right.

13.4   FR236 to left, just past farm buildings. The forest road resembles a driveway for the farm, but like all forest roads, it has a stop sign with a forest road number. FR236 leads uphill to a parking area and the trailhead of the Tolliver Tr.

Page Valley Rd continues for two more miles to a dead end.

Waterlick - Bentonville (SR678, SR619, SR613)

These numbered routes connect the crossroad community known as Waterlick with the small town of Bentonville and provide access to four trails on the north end of Massanutten Mountain. Most of the land along the roads is privately owned.

South	North	
0.0	**11.7**	Waterlick. At junction of VA55 and SR678, 5 mi west of US340-522 near Front Royal, and 5 mi east of US11 in Strasburg.
1.2	**10.5**	Southbound, turn left, onto SR619. Northbound, turn right, onto SR678.
1.5	**10.2**	Virginia Fish Cultural Station, where fish are taught which fork (of the river) to use when dining.
2.4	**9.3**	Buzzard Rock Tr, parking lot (8), west.
4.3	**7.4**	Junction of SR619 with SR613, Panhandle Rd. Southbound, turn right onto SR613. Northbound, turn left. Road surface change: north paved, south gravel.
4.8	**6.9**	Road surface change: north gravel, south paved.
5.8	**5.9**	Forest road, west, leads to the trailhead of the Shawl Gap Tr in a loop parking area (6). Road may be rutted. This turn is not signed, and is easy to miss; when driving south, watch for a road sign that signals a change in the road surface.
5.9	**5.8**	Road surface changes: north paved and wide, south gravel and narrow.

7.0   4.7   Sherman Gap Tr, pink-blazed, west. Trail ascends a rutted forest road, just south of private property. This trailhead is easy to miss. Parking (2) is difficult.

8.9   2.8   Tuscarora Tr, blue-blazed, intersects road west, at a bend in road. Dirt driveway leads to parking (8). Southbound, blue blazes run along the road.

10.5   1.2   Sharp bend in road where a private road, closed, leads south. Changes in road name and surface: Panhandle Rd, gravel, north; Indian Hollow Rd, paved, south.

10.7   1.0   Midpoint of Indian Hollow Bridge over the Shenandoah South Fork, a one-lane, low-water bridge.

10.8   0.9   Tuscarora Tr, blue-blazed, intersects road, south. Westbound, blue blazes run along the road. Eastbound, silver blazes on trees along the road indicate "no hunting."

11.7   0.0   Junction of SR613 with US340, just south of center of Bentonville. Front Royal is 9.5 mi to north, Luray is 14 mi to south.

Forest Roads

Big Mountain Rd (FR375)

This forest road begins from Cub Run Rd, near Catherine Furnace, rises steeply through the gorge drained by Pitt Spring Run, then rises gradually between Big Mountain and Massanutten Mountain. (FR375 is also called TV Tower Rd, and Pitt Spring Rd.) Some hunter campsites along the road.

North

0.0   On Cub Run Rd, FR65. See separate road approach, Cub Run Rd, below. Drive west on FR375.

0.1   A gated forest road goes right and intersects Roaring Run Trail in 1.4 mi. Just beyond, pass through gate on FR375, which may be locked if road has deteriorated due to severe weather. CAUTION: many sharp dips ahead in the road surface to control runoff. These are abupt and deceptive when driving north.

1.2   Cross Pitt Spring Run on narrow bridge.

1.4   Recross Pitt Spring Run on a culvert.

1.7   Massanutten South Tr, orange-blazed, joins road from west. Parking (5) at bend in road. Footbridge over the run leads to Pitt Spring. Continue north, with orange blazes along road.

2.6   Powerline for TV tower joins road from east.

3.6   Buried gas line crosses.

4.5   Roaring Run Tr, purple-blazed, east. Parking (4) along road.

4.9   Bird Knob Tr, white-blazed, goes west on gated forest road. Parking (4).

5.3   FR375 turns sharply right to ascend past locked gate to TV tower. Massanutten South Tr continues north on gated woods road. Parking (3), but do not block either gate.

Crisman Hollow Rd (FR274)

This forest road starts in New Market Gap and ascends along the east slope of Kerns Mountain to a saddle between Kerns and Waterfall Mountains, then gradually descends northward, into Crisman Hollow, along Passage Creek. Many hunter campsites.

North   South

0.0   9.2   New Market Gap on US211. See separate road approach, Luray – New Market (above). FR274 begins paved.

1.5   7.7   Massanutten Story Book Trail, east. Parking (12). Surface change: gravel north, paved south.

2.2   7.0   High point of road (a saddle). Massanutten Tr (east CCW 36.8, west CW 34.3), orange-blazed, crosses.

4.5   4.7   Scothorn Gap Tr, yellow-blazed, east. Parking (4) along the trail itself, before the creek.

6.2   3.0   Gap Creek Tr, blue-blazed, east. A parking loop (8) east of road – trail begins as part of loop.

6.3   2.9   Jawbone Gap Tr, blue-blazed, west. Parking (3) along road.

6.5   2.7   Cross Passage Creek on a large culvert.

8.3   0.9   Lion's Tale Tr, west. Restrooms. Parking lot (15).

9.2   0.0   Junction of FR274, SR730, and SR675. See separate road approaches, Moreland Gap Rd, and Edinburg – Luray. Southbound, FR274 begins as a gravel surface.

Cub Run Forest Rd (FR65)

This north-south forest road, FR65, runs along the east slope of the southern half of the Massanutten and is the primary access to most of the trails. FR65 is accessed on the south from SR636, and on the north from SR685.

North   South

0.0   14.3   SR636, Runkles Gap Rd, west of SR602. (This is 3.9 mi southwest from a traffic light in the center of the town of Shenandoah, and 4.4 mi northeast of US33.) Turn west on SR636, paved.

2.1   12.2   Name change: Northbound, road becomes Cub Run Rd, FR65, gravel, Forest Service maintenance. Southbound, road becomes Runkles Gap Rd, SR636, paved, state maintenance.

2.3   12.0   FR65A, gated, north. Northbound, pass through a gate on FR65, usually open. Massanutten South Tr, orange-blazed, begins at the gate and follows the road through Runkles Gap. Parking along road (6).

2.6   11.7   Massanutten South Tr, orange-blazed, leaves west at a bend in the road. Parking along road (6) east of this bend.

4.0   10.3   Top of rise near Peterfish Gap. Fridley Gap Tr, purple-blazed, west, just north of a gated forest road. Parking (5) along road. Begin descent in either direction.

5.4   8.9   Cub Run passes under road through culvert.

5.5   8.6   Martins Bottom Tr, blue-blazed, west, on a wide forest road. Parking (3) along road.

8.4   5.9   Cross low-water bridge over Morgan Run.

8.5   5.8   Morgan Run Tr, yellow-blazed, west. Parking (3) along road.

11.2   3.1   Cross low-water bridge over Pitt Spring Run. Big Mountain Rd to west. See separate road approach, Big Mountain Rd (FR375), above.

11.5   2.8   Catherine Furnace, west of road, near low-water bridge over Roaring Run. Just north of bridge, Roaring Run Tr, purple-blazed, starts west on blocked dirt road. Parking (6) at Catherine Furnace area.

11.9   2.4   Intersection of Katherine Furnace Rd (which becomes Cub Run Rd as road enters national forest and changes to dirt surface) and SR685, Newport Rd. SR685 is paved and makes a sharp turn at this intersection. Northbound traffic (exiting from FR65) should turn left.

14.3   0.0   Town of Newport on US340 (4.1 mi south of US211 and 7.3 mi north of town of Shenandoah). Traffic for Cub Run Rd should turn west on SR685, Newport Rd, next to a general store.

Edinburg Gap Forest Rd (FR374)

This forest road connects SR730 in Moreland Gap with SR675 in Edinburg Gap. The wide gravel surface, with moderate grades, runs along the east slope of Short Mountain.

South   North

0.0   5.8   Edinburg Gap. See separate road approach, Edinburg – Luray. The Massanutten Tr crosses SR675 here (south CCW 22.4, north CW 48.7). Southbound, FR374 is the right fork; the left fork leads to parking (10) and a maze of ATV trails. Massanutten Tr's orange blazes along FR374.

0.4   5.4   Massanutten Tr (west into woods CCW 22.8, north on road CW 48.3), orange-blazed. Parking (4) on east edge of road.

4.8   1.0   Massanutten Tr (east CCW 29.5, west CW 41.6), orange-blazed, crosses. Parking (2) on east edge of road.

5.8   0.0   Junction of FR374 with SR730, Moreland Gap Rd. See separate road approach, Moreland Gap Rd, above. Parking (5) here for Massanutten Tr, which crosses Moreland Gap Rd 0.1 mi to east.

Powells Fort Camp (FR66)

FR66 runs north between Green Mountain and Three Top Mountain in a little valley that parallels Fort Valley. FR66 goes all the way to Signal Knob but is always locked just north of Powells Fort Camp. There are some hunter campsites south of the gate, but camping is not allowed at Powells Fort Camp, which is closed.

**Approaching from the south, using the Detrick –
Woodstock Rd approach.**

0.0   Junction of FR273 with SR758, Woodstock Tower Rd.
Drive north on FR273, gravel surfaced, passing through Mine
Mountain Estates area (private).

2.4   Junction of FR66 with FR273, where FR273 swings
east. Continue at **FR66 North**, below.

**Approaching from the east, using Fort Valley Rd
approach.**

0.0   Junction of SR771, Boyer Rd with SR678, Fort Valley
Rd. Drive west on SR771, gravel surfaced after the turn.

1.0   Fork in road, SR771 swings left. Go straight onto
FR273. Pass through water gap in Green Mountain with Mine
Run in ravine to left of road.

1.6   Junction of FR66 with FR273, where FR273 swings
south. Turn right and continue below.

FR66 North.

0.0   FR66 is gated here. This gate is normally open, but
may be locked due to storm damage.

0.1   Mine Gap Tr, purple-blazed, left. Parking (6) right, in
50 yds.

1.9   Southern entrance (gated) to Powells Fort Camp, left.
Massanutten Tr (west off road CCW 9.0, north on road CW
62.1), orange-blazed, enters the road from left and continues
along road, straight ahead. (Powells Fort Camp is closed, and is
used only for special events. No camping.) Parking (3) off
road, or in a parking-and-turn-around area (7) left of road
about 0.1 mi farther north.

2.3   Mudhole Gap Tr, purple-blazed, right, begins as a
forest road. Parking area (10) on trail may be muddy in wet
weather. Northern entrance (gated) to Powells Fort Camp, west
side, is nearby. Do not block gate.

2.4   Locked gate. FR66 continues north to the Strasburg
Reservoir and the TV tower on Signal Knob. It is also the route
of the Massanutten Tr. Reliable piped spring, west side, just
before the gate.

3. The Massanutten Trail

THE north half of the Massanutten is a 28-mile long system of ridges and valleys, about six miles wide. Down the center of the Massanutten's ridge system there is a broad, rolling inner valley known as Fort Valley. Most of Fort Valley is privately owned farmland, but the mountain ridges surrounding it are in the George Washington National Forest.

The orange-blazed Massanutten Trail (MT), dedicated in 2002, circles Fort Valley, mostly on the ridges. There are peaks, knobs, towers, overlooks, and in some places an almost continual view along this 71-mile circuit. Other trails run parallel to the MT, and serve as alternate paths. Still more trails climb from nearby roads to the ridges.

George Washington surveyed a circuit on the Massanutten for Lord Fairfax, about 1748-9. The survey started in Passage Creek gorge below Buzzard Rock at a ford called Slippery Rock. The line went west to the Lickliter Branch, also called Fox Grape River at that time. This had to be Little Passage Creek since there is no other stream west of Buzzard Rock. The line then followed the stream through Mudhole Gap back to Passage Creek. The line crossed Passage Creek at a beaver dam and took an easterly course to Four Pile Corner at the top of Page Mountain (Massanutten Mountain) at the north end of Little Crease Mountain. This is the only place where the bends and ridges in the mountain can be construed as a place of four corners. The line then went north along the ridge to Buzzard Rock.

Hikers on the Massanutten Trail between Buzzard Rock and Sherman Gap will be walking in Washington's footsteps.

The MT passes near a reservoir, three Forest Service developed campgrounds, one three-sided shelter, and many dispersed campsites. Water sources are infrequent, so careful planning is required. All water sources should be purified before being consumed and before being used to wash eating utensils.

The MT crosses county roads or forest system roads at ten points. The diagram of Road Access Points on page 30 shows these crossings in relation to major highways and also shows the

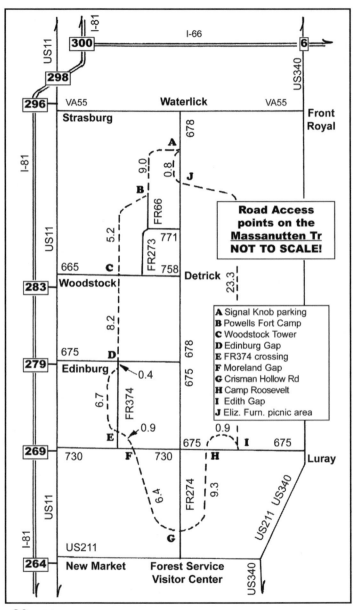

Road Access points on the Massanutten Tr NOT TO SCALE!

A Signal Knob parking
B Powells Fort Camp
C Woodstock Tower
D Edinburg Gap
E FR374 crossing
F Moreland Gap
G Crisman Hollow Rd
H Camp Roosevelt
I Edith Gap
J Eliz. Furn. picnic area

trail mileage between the crossings. Thanks to the road crossings, hikers using two vehicles can backpack the circuit in weekend segments. Many day-hike and overnight circuits are possible using side trails and a segment of the MT. Detailed mileage diagrams and descriptions of all the side trails are provided in the Elizabeth Furnace, West, East, and Crisman Hollow trail groups.

The United States Forest Service has recognized the Massanutten Trail as a National Recreation Trail in the National Trails System.

Two descriptions are supplied for the MT, one clockwise (CW), the other counterclockwise (CCW). Each description supplies complete information for a thru-hike. Each description begins at the Signal Knob parking area on Fort Valley Rd at the north end of Fort Valley. Be sure to read *Camping in the National Forest* in Chapter 1.

When using a segment of the MT in a shorter circuit hike, you will need to choose one of the descriptions based on your hiking direction. To simplify the problem of intersecting a trail that runs in a closed loop, each description of a road approach or a side trail specifies which MT description should be used. For example, the road approach Edinburg-Luray crosses the MT at three locations. At the Camp Roosevelt crossing (**H** in the road access diagram), the road approach describes the crossing as:

9.7   8.2 Massanutten Tr (north CCW 46.1, south CW 25.0)...

If you plan to hike south into Duncan Hollow, you will need to use the MT CW description, starting at milepoint 25.0.

The Massanutten Trail Clockwise (CW)

Miles

0   At the north end of the Signal Knob parking lot. [740] If hiking through this point, bear right to stay on the trail, which runs parallel to the parking lot. If starting from this point, take a short unblazed trail from the south end of the parking lot that joins the MT at milepoint 0.2.

0.2   Unblazed trail joins from south end of the parking lot.

0.3   Join a wagon road running parallel to Fort Valley Rd.

0.6   Tuscarora Tr, Bear Wallow section, blue-blazed, joins from the right. [900] There is a large campsite to the right on the Tuscarora in 70 yds. Turn left, blue and orange blazes. *You are entering the Passage Creek Day Use area where camping is prohibited except in the developed campgrounds.* Camping is permitted again beyond milepoint 1.1. Descend on an eroded ore road across shale barren. Watch for bits of furnace slag that were used to surface the road in 1800s.

0.8   Fort Valley Rd, SR678. (There is a hand-pump for water, available year-round, at the Elizabeth Furnace Family Campground, 0.4 mi south along the left shoulder of the road, see map.) Cross SR678, descend, turn right on a paved entry road, cross bridge.

0.9   End of concrete bridge. [740] (50 yds farther on the paved road, right, in the picnic area there are restrooms, trash bins and a water spigot May to October, but no camping.) The water in Passage Creek is not recommended, since it has flowed past many miles of home and pasture drainage, and under numerous road crossings.

          The MT drops left off the road surface and follows the creek downstream, then bears away from the creek.

1.0   Ruins of Elizabeth Furnace, right. The Pig Iron and Charcoal interpretive trails (Chapter 10) start near the furnace. Trail bears away from the creek and gets steeper. Begin ascent [+970] of the west face of Massanutten Mountain on switchbacks.

1.1   Switchback left at the edge of an old wagon road. *End of the restricted camping area.*
1.5   Cross old wagon road.
1.7   At a bend left, an unblazed trail continues south to a view of Fort Valley. Trail ahead is rocky with flights of steps.
2.9   Cross old wagon road. An unreliable rock-lined spring at this intersection. Large, tipped rocks ahead in the tread.
3.0   Shawl Gap. [1710] Campsite. Shawl Gap Tr, yellow-blazed, straight ahead. Buzzard Rock Tr, white-blazed, left. Potential tentsites nearby along Buzzard Rock Tr, and a unique campsite on a knob in about 0.4 mi.
          Turn right, ascend [+270] on very rocky tread.
3.4   High point of ridge [1980]. Rocky tread ahead [1900 to 2180].
4.5   Tread becomes less rocky.
5.3   Sherman Gap Tr, pink-blazed, joins from right. Steep descent ahead. Orange, blue, and pink blazes!
5.4   Sherman Gap Tr leaves left [1960], ascend [+300] in next 0.2 mi, then trail follows twisting ridge where Massanutten and Little Crease mountains join.
6.4   View east to Shenandoah National Park on Blue Ridge.
6.5   Bear right off the ridge [2080], descend [-900] on switchbacks, entering drainage area between Massanutten and Little Crease mountains. (A bushwhack straight ahead along the ridge of Massanutten Mountain for 1.5 mi will intersect the MT at milepoint 9.7.)
8.2   Campsite on unblazed path left, △.
8.7   Veach Gap Tr, yellow-blazed, right, on Morgan's Rd as it comes through the gap from Fort Valley. [1180] The road was built by Daniel Morgan under orders from George Washington, who was anticipating a possible retreat to Fort Valley as a winter encampment for the Continental Army. Cross Mill Run.
8.8   Little Crease Shelter, left, busy on weekends. Tentsites nearby. Reliable spring. *This is last reliable water for 16 mi.* Continue on Morgan's Rd, [+600] in next mile.

9.7   On ridge, bear right. [1780] Tuscarora Tr (Veach Gap section) leaves left on Morgan's Rd, to cross the valley and meet the Appalachian Trail in Shenandoah National Park. Walk a short distance down the Tuscarora as it descends to appreciate this well-built, 240-year-old road cut into the side of the mountain.

9.8   Large campsite [1800]. Ridge ahead [1800 to 2000].

12.1   The MT bears left, off the ridge, on a narrow footpath called the Billy Goat section. Good views east. A wide, unblazed route continues south along the ridge, but on the edge of private property.

12.7   The MT rejoins the ridge south of private property.

13.2   Milford Gap Tr, white-blazed, left only. [1760] Small campsite on the ridge, left.

13.5   Multi-tent campsite, left [1840].

14.3   Unblazed wagon road right, leads to private property.

14.6   Indian Grave Ridge Tr, purple-blazed, left. [1980] Saw-tooth ridge ahead [1900 to 2100], good views, rocky tread.

18.1   Habron Gap Tr, blue-blazed, left. [1930] There is a campsite, 0.2 mi [-120] down Habron Gap Tr. Cache. The unblazed wagon road right leads to private property.

20.8   Stephens Tr, yellow-blazed, right. [2150] For 250 yds ahead, the ridge is flat and wide, one campsite and potential tentsites.

21.7   Kennedy Peak Tr, white-blazed, left [2380], [+220] to peak. The stone base of an old fire tower on the peak [2600] has a wooden floor and a wooden observation deck above. The enclosed space forms a mini-shelter (for one or two) on the highest point along the ridge. No space for tents, however.

The MT begins to circle Kennedy Peak on its west slope.

21.8   An unblazed loop trail, right, for a limited view into Fort Valley. Farther on, a well-worn unblazed trail leaves left from a sharp switchback right. It goes to the base of a former microwave tower on the steep, east slope of Kennedy Peak. No campsites, tentsites, water, or views.

22.5 Join wide roadbed, open to 4WD vehicles to this point. There are a half dozen vehicle campsites along this 4WD ridge road, most near the Edith Gap end.

24.1 Edith Gap, SR675. [1850] Hang-gliding from this point when winds cooperate. Turn right on road, then right off the road to descend [-550] on switchbacks, passing a pit mine. A deep V-cut in the upslope on the left leads to the bottom of the pit.

24.9 Forest Service shed. Stephens Tr, yellow-blazed, begins right, through parking lot. Turn left on entrance road.

25.0 SR675 again. [1300] Camp Roosevelt picnic area is 130 yds to the right on SR675. For water from May to October, follow unblazed path right into picnic area, bubbler, trash bins, restrooms. Cache in winter.

Cross SR675, gentle descent, crossing shale barrens.

25.1 Large campsite right where an old wagon road crosses. Farther on, a small bridge over a drain.

25.4 Cross unreliable creek that drains Duncan Hollow. [1300] (The creek may be dry here, but becomes reliable farther south.) Climb bank, large campsite. Bear left onto a wide wagon road that parallels the creek.

25.6 Large campsite, left, unreliable creek behind it.

27.9 Unique campsite, left, beside reliable creek, △.

28.2 Two crossings of reliable creek.

28.3 Gap Creek Tr, blue-blazed, right. [1870] Large campsite left, △, on unblazed trail across reliable creek. The unblazed trail continues to private property. The Gap Creek and Jawbone Gap trails provide an alternate 2.6 mi route to milepoint 31.0, passing a spur trail to Duncan Knob enroute.

The MT begins to angle up the east slope of Middle Mountain [+850], drawing away from the creek.

30.1 Cross ridge of Middle Mtn. [2720]. Begin angled descent of the west face of Middle Mountain.

31.0 Scothorn Gap Tr, yellow-blazed, on a saddle between Waterfall and Middle mountains. [2500] Each trail makes a right angled turn. Straight ahead on Scothorn Gap Tr there are an unreliable spring right at 120 yds; three large campsites at 500, 600, and 630 yds; and many tentsites.

The MT turns left, ascends a little, then descends [-900] into the steep-sided drainage system of Big Run, reliable. Cross the drainage to the west. The trail is generally on narrow sidehill tread above the run, and crossings of the run are slippery. Recross the run to the east; join an old wagon road.

32.9 Cross Big Run to west. [1600] *This is last reliable water for 15 miles.* Two-tent campsite between the trail and the run.

33.1 Massanutten Connector Tr, white-blazed, straight ahead. [1500] Turn right, ascend [+900] on steep switchbacks, stone steps at the top.

33.7 Ridge of Waterfall Mountain [2400]. The MT turns left, south, along the ridge, through fields of blueberry. Watch for bears when berries are ripe.

34.1 Pass an overlook, with a view east around Strickler Knob and across the valley of the South Fork. Then bear right away from the ridge, on a gentle descent through old clearings.

34.3 Crisman Hollow Rd, FR274, on a high saddle between Waterfall and Kerns mountains. [2330] Cache. Cross road, ascend [+120]. Campsite in 100 yds.

Nearing the top, swing right onto the broad, flat sandy ridge of Kerns Mountain, [2450 to 2550]. Potential tentsites. The ridge narrows and becomes very rocky going north and camping becomes impossible. The trail alternates between short sections on the narrow ridge and longer sections along the slope on either side of the ridge. There are short, steep sections (sometimes switchbacked), to get between the ridge and the sideslope sections. One 200-ft section on the west slope passes along rock outcrops that are covered with leathery lichen and topped with dense mats of common polypody fern, green year-round. Good views on the highest points.

39.1 Jawbone Gap. [2400] Jawbone Gap Tr, blue-blazed, right. White-blazed spur trail straight ahead ascends for 200 yds [+120] to Jawbone Overlook. Charred stumps along this trail are the remains of a 10,000 acre fire in 1980. The overlook offers a long, narrow view to the west between Kerns and Short mountains and a wide view to the east to Duncan Knob across Crisman Hollow.

Turn left, descend the west slope of Kerns Mountain on a steep, switchbacked wagon road. There are several unreliable springs in the upslope along the lower sections.

39.5   Bear right off the wagon road onto a narrow sidehill path, very rocky in places, then join grassy logging road.

40.7   Moreland Gap Rd, SR730, on a saddle between Kerns and Short mountains. [1890] Cache. Cross SR730 onto a narrow path.

40.8   Bear right onto a wide coaling road, grassy.

41.1   Unreliable stream, which has passed through a culvert under FR374, crosses trail. Single tentsites to the right, △, both before and after the stream.

41.4   Paired tentsites to the left, △, on a charcoal hearth, below FR374.

41.6   FR374 [2040]. Cache. Cross the road, ascend [+600] the east face of Short Mountain on rocky, switchbacked tread, below rock outcrops near the top.

42.5   Turn right along rocky ridge [2650 to 2750]. Nice view east before the trail moves under trees.

45.4   Fire ring (only) in a low wooded area. Unblazed access trails, right to FR374, left to private property. Ahead, occasional sitting walls.

46.9   High point. Begin descent [-1000] to Edinburg Gap.

47.4   Overlook on the nose of Short Mountain [~2500], with a panoramic view north along the spine of Powell Mountain, the Shenandoah North Fork valley to the left with Great North Mountain on the horizon. Continue to descend on twisting narrow trail, occasional views left of Waonaze Peak.

48.1   Old coaling road crosses the trail on a charcoal hearth. Two pairs of tentsites, △, to the right along this old road.

48.3   FR374. Cache. Turn left, descend along FR374.

48.7   SR675. Edinburg Gap. [1690] Restroom at the back end of the ATV parking area, right.

There is a reliable piped spring at a pull-off along SR675, 0.5 mi [-140] to the east of the mountain on SR675. *Caution: SR675 has narrow travel lanes, no shoulders, two blind curves, and drivers do not expect to see pedestrians.*

Cross SR675, then bear left off the Peters Mill Run Tr (an ATV/OHV road, with yellow V-blazes).

Ascend [+1000] in next 1.6 miles.

49.5 Unreliable piped spring with a sign, left.

49.8 Potential tentsites, left, as trail bears left into a gently sloped area with huge stone blocks.

50.3 View east into Fort Valley at Kings Crossing. Continue near the ridge of Powell Mountain [1850 to 2000].

50.4 Unblazed trail left leads to highest point of Waonaze Peak [2700], with view to west.

50.9 Bear Trap Tr, pink-blazed, right. [2360]

51.4 Unblazed trail left leads to an overlook with view of the valley north of Edinburg. Known informally as Bill Kruszka's Overlook, in remembrance of the retired Forest Service employee who laid out much of the MT and guided PATC's Massarock Crew many summers.

53.6 7-Bar None Tr, blue-blazed, right. [1840] Large campsite. Unreliable water in Peters Mill Run 0.4 mi [-200] down this steep trail. The unblazed trail left leads to private property.

55.0 Lupton Tr, purple-blazed, right. [1800] Unreliable water in Peters Mill Run 0.4 mi [-340] down this steep trail.

55.1 Cross to west of the ridge, descend, and join a rocky wagon road that parallels the ridge.

56.7 Hang-glider launch site, busy when winds cooperate.

56.9 Woodstock Tower Rd, SR758. [1850] The Woodstock Tower is up on the ridge. To access it, ascend on SR758 to a short pink-blazed trail. The tower affords a panoramic view of the Seven Bends of the Shenandoah, with Great North Mountain on the horizon.

Cache. (A reliable piped spring is located 1.1 miles from here. Using the inset on map G, and trail descriptions, follow Wagon Rd Tr [-500], to Little Fort Campground, turn left on campground road, pass campsites 9 and 10 and bear right onto a fork in the entrance road. Follow road to parking for picnic area, angle left 75 yds across grassy field, cross a wooden bridge over Peters Mill Run, walk 50 yds farther to low concrete structure. Pipe comes out the far side.)

57.2   Cross SR758 and descend to continue on a wagon road that parallels the ridge of Three Top Mountain.

57.2   Two short sections of rock bridging across gullies.

57.5   Former hang-glider launch site. Nice view.

58.2   End of wagon road, ascend on narrower trail to the ridge, then continue north on the ridge [1700 to 1900].

60.4   Mine Gap Tr, purple-blazed, right. [1770] A two-tent campsite left, △, 50 yds before the intersection.

61.6   Tuscarora Tr (Doll Ridge section), blue-blazed, merges from left [1770] and runs concurrent for 35 yds, then angles upslope to the ridge of Three Top Mountain, providing an alternate path to 65.4 for those who like a rocky ridge trail. The MT angles down the east face of Three Top Mountain [-500] into Little Fort Valley.

62.1   FR66. Powells Fort Camp, south entrance road left, gated. [1270] *Powells Fort Camp area is closed and camping is not allowed between the south and north entrance roads.* Also, camping is not recommended along this driveable part of FR66. The MT continues north on FR66, almost flat.

62.2   Parking and turnaround area on left.

62.5   Mudhole Gap Tr, purple-blazed, right. [1200] North entrance road, gated, to Powells Fort Camp, left. The south-flowing Little Passage Creek turns east here to flow through Mudhole Gap and join the north-flowing Passage Creek in Fort Valley.

62.6   Reliable piped spring left. Continue on FR66, passing a locked gate.

62.8   Large campsite, △, in a clearing right, with tentsites under pines near reliable creek.

63.7   Cross Little Passage Creek, reliable.

64.5   The MT bears left off the road to skirt the west shore of the Strasburg Reservoir. *The reservoir is on private property and is not developed for public use.*

65.1   Trail rejoins FR66, continuing north.

65.4   Tuscarora Tr, blue-blazed, crosses. [1550] There is a large campsite 40 yds right on Tuscarora, then, △, 100 yds north on an unblazed path. The Tuscarora, Bear Wallow section (to the right), and the Meneka Peak trails provide an alternate path to 67.7.

Ahead, between the road and the creek, there are liming stations, where finely ground limestone is dumped into

Block field on Massanutten Trail (by Lee Sheaffer)

the creek to control the acidity of the water. Last reliable water here in creek for next 7 miles. Ascend [+450] on steep roadbed.

66.5   As road bends right near the top, MT bears left onto a narrow path.

66.6   Signal Knob Overlook. [2100] View of the northern Shenandoah Valley toward Winchester. The north fork of the river (hidden from view) turns east around the end of the mountain, is joined by Passage Creek as it flows north from Fort Valley, then joins the south fork at Riverton, near Front Royal, then continues north to the Potomac at Harpers Ferry.

Turn east on a level path. Small campsites and tentsites, busy on weekends. Rejoin FR66, pass the TV tower, and enter a wide, wooded path, almost level, as it bears left along the rim of a steep-sided depression, then ascends and crosses the nose of Green Mountain [2240] on very rocky tread.

67.7   Meneka Peak Tr, white-blazed. [2200] There is a campsite on the right, 310 yds south on Meneka Peak Tr.

67.8   Large campsite left.

67.9   Small campsite left. Tread begins to cross a series of block fields.

68.9   Fort Valley Overlook. [1800] More block fields.

69.6   Buzzard Rock Overlook. [1540] (Buzzard Rock is east, across Passage Creek gorge.) Begin [-800] descent to Fort Valley Rd, occasionally rocky.

70.7   Sharp turn left in a ravine with a piped spring, unreliable.

70.9   A stone cabin (locked) above the trail is a Forest Service administrative building.

71.1   A wooden bridge at the north end of the Signal Knob parking area. [740] If hiking through, bear right to stay on the blazed trail, which runs parallel to the parking lot.

The Massanutten Trail Counterclockwise (CCW)

Miles

0   North end of the Signal Knob Parking lot. [740] Hike north. Ascend [+800] in next 1.5 mi, occasionally rocky.

0.2   A stone cabin (locked) above the trail is a Forest Service administrative building.

0.4   Sharp turn right in a ravine with a spring, unreliable.

1.5   Buzzard Rock Overlook. [1540] (Buzzard Rock is east, across Passage Creek gorge.) Block fields ahead.

Signal Knob from approach on Massanutten Trail (by Lee Sheaffer)

2.2   Fort Valley Overlook. [1800] More block fields ahead.

3.2   Campsite right.

3.3   Larger campsite right.

3.4   Meneka Peak Tr, white-blazed. [2200] There is a campsite on the right 310 yds south on Meneka Peak Tr. The Meneka Peak and Tuscarora trails provide an alternate path to milepoint 5.7. Rocky footing ahead where the MT crosses the nose of Green Mountain [2240], then descends.

3.8   Tread is flat, less rocky, circles a steep-sided depression on right.

4.4   Television tower, *not* the Signal Knob Overlook! Pass the tower site, then bear right off the gravel road onto a level path, passing small campsites and tentsites, busy on weekends.

4.5   Signal Knob Overlook. [2100] View of the northern Shenandoah Valley toward Winchester. The north fork of the river turns east (hidden from view) around the end of the mountain, is joined by Passage Creek as it exits from Fort Valley, then joins the south fork near Front Royal, and continues north to the Potomac at Harpers Ferry. Great North Mountain, on the left horizon, defines the West Virginia border.

Continue south on a path from the overlook, then join FR66. Descend into Little Fort Valley [-450] between Green and Three Top mountains. Steep, with loose gravel. Little Passage Creek begins in springs east of the road. The creek is a reliable water source, but in dry weather you may have to go almost to 5.7 to find water. Piles of finely ground limestone are dumped along the creek in various places to reduce the acidity of the water.

5.7   Tuscarora Tr, blue-blazed, crosses, Bear Wallow section left, Doll Ridge section right. [1550] For a large campsite, go left on the Tuscarora for 40 yds, then △,100 yds north on an unblazed path. The Doll Ridge section provides an alternate path to milepoint 9.5, for those who like a rocky ridge trail. The MT continues on FR66.

6.0   Bear right off FR66 onto a narrow path that skirts the west shore of the Strasburg Reservoir, reliable. *The reservoir is* *on private property and is not developed for public use.* Cross Little Passage Creek, reliable, below the reservoir.

6.6   Rejoin FR66, continuing south.

7.4   Cross Little Passage Creek, reliable. Little Passage Creek flows south through Little Fort Valley, whereas Passage Creek flows north through Fort Valley.

8.3   Large campsite in clearing left △, with tentsites under pines near reliable creek.

8.5   Locked gate. FR66 is driveable to this gate, camping is not recommended south of the gate. Piped spring right just beyond the gate, reliable. Next reliable water is a mile off the MT at milepoint 14.2.

8.6   Powells Fort Camp, north entrance road right, gated. Powells Fort Camp is closed and camping is not allowed in the camp between the north and south entrance roads. Just south of here is Mudhole Gap Tr, purple-blazed, left. Little Passage Creek turns east here through Mudhole Gap in Green Mountain.

8.9   Road right to a turnaround and parking area.

9.0   Powells Fort Camp, south entrance road right, gated. [1270] Bear right off FR66 onto a narrow woods path. Angle up the east face of Three Top Mountain [+500].

9.5   Tuscarora Tr, blue-blazed, merges from right and runs concurrent for 35 yds [1770], then bears right to cross Three Top Mountain and descend on Doll Ridge. The MT bears left along Three Top Mountain, near the ridge.

10.7   Mine Gap Tr, purple-blazed. [1770] A two-tent campsite, right, △, in 50 yds. Trail ahead skirts rocky sections of the ridge [1700 to 1900].

12.9   Brief descent from the ridge on the west face to join an old wagon road that parallels the ridgetop.

13.6   Former hang glider launch site. Nice view.

13.9   Two short sections of rock bridging across gulleys.

14.2   Woodstock Tower Rd, SR758. [1850] The Woodstock Tower is up on the ridge. To access it, ascend on road, then follow short pink-blazed trail. The tower affords a panoramic view of the Seven Bends of the Shenandoah, with Great North Mountain on the horizon.

Cache. (A reliable piped spring is located 1.1 miles from here. Using the inset on map G, and trail descriptions, follow Wagon Rd Tr [-500], to Little Fort Campground, turn left on campground road, pass campsites 9 and 10 and bear right onto a fork in the entrance road. Follow road to parking for picnic area, angle left 75 yds across grassy field, cross a wooden bridge over Peters Mill Run, walk 50 yds farther to a low concrete structure. Pipe comes out the far side.)

Cross SR758, and join a wagon road along the west face of Powell Mountain near the ridge, rocky in places.

14.4   Hang glider launch site, busy when winds cooperate.

16.0   Cross Powell Mountain ridge to east.

16.1   Lupton Tr, purple-blazed, left. [1800] Unreliable water in Peters Mill Run 0.4 mi [-340] down this steep trail.

17.5   7-Bar None Tr, blue-blazed, left. [1840] Campsite in this intersection. Unreliable water in Peters Mill Run 0.4 mi [-200] down this steep trail. The unblazed trail to the right leads to private property.

19.7   Unblazed trail right leads to overlook with a view of the valley north of Edinburg. Known informally as Bill Kruszka's Overlook, in remembrance of the retired Forest Service employee who laid out much of the MT and guided PATC's Massarock Crew many summers.

20.2   Bear Trap Tr, pink-blazed, left. [2360] Gradual climb ahead.

20.7   Unblazed trail, right, leads to high point of Waonaze Peak [2700], with view to west.

20.8   View east into Fort Valley at Kings Crossing. Begin descent [-1000] to milepoint 22.4. Switchbacks. Interesting broken rock formations.

21.3   Potential tentsites, right, in a gently sloped area with large stone blocks, just before bearing right onto narrow sidehill tread.

21.6   Unreliable piped spring with sign, right.

22.4   SR675. Edinburg Gap. [1690] The MT joins the Peters Mill Run Tr (OHV) just before meeting SR675. The Peters Mill Run Tr has ATV and OHV traffic and SR675 has normal vehicular traffic. *This can be a dangerous intersection.*

There is a reliable piped spring at a pull-off along SR675, 0.5 mi [-140] to the east. *Caution: SR675 has narrow travel lanes, blind curves, no shoulders, and drivers do not expect to see a pedestrian.*

Cross SR675. Restroom in back of the ATV parking area. Bear right to follow blazes up FR374, Edinburg Gap Forest Rd. Begin gradual climb of 1000 feet to 25.1.

22.8   Turn right off FR374 onto rising tread. Cache.

23.0   Old coaling road crosses the MT on a charcoal hearth. Two pairs of tentsites, △, in woods left along this old road. The MT twists and turns, almost boxing the compass as it winds between FR374 and the north end of Short Mountain. At one point, it is on a narrow ledge cut into a very steep cross slope below rock outcrops. Occasional views of Waonaze Peak, right.

23.6   Overlook on the nose of Short Mountain. [2500] Panoramic view back along the spine of Powell Mountain, across Woodstock and the North Fork of the Shenandoah, with Great North Mountain on the left horizon. Bear left around the nose of Short Mountain and ascend near rising ridge.

25.1   High point, continue on ridge [2650 to 2750], with dips east or west to avoid rocky outcrops. Occasional sitting walls.

25.7   Fire ring (only) in a low wooded area. Unblazed access trails, left to FR374, right to private property.

28.6   Overlook east past Kennedy Peak to the Blue Ridge. Swing left, descend east face of Short Mountain [-600] on narrow, steep sidehill tread below rock outcrops. One switchback. Less steep in a wooded section with seeps before reaching the road.

29.5   FR374, Edinburg Gap Forest Rd. [2040] Cache. Cross FR374 onto a wide logging road then right onto a narrow path.

29.7   Paired tentsites right, △, on a charcoal hearth below FR374. Then join a wide coaling road.

30.0 An unreliable stream, which has passed through a culvert under FR374, crosses. Single tentsites left, △, both before and after crossing the stream.

30.3 Bear left off the wagon road onto a narrow path.

30.4 Moreland Gap Rd, SR730 [1890], on a saddle between Kerns and Short mountains. Cache. Cross SR730. Ascend [+510] west face of Kerns Mountain. Grassy logging road, then rocky path.

31.6 Join an old wagon road, begin four steep switchbacks. A few unreliable springs along the lower switchbacks.

32.0 Jawbone Gap. [2400] Jawbone Gap Tr, blue-blazed, descends east. A white-blazed spur trail ascends left for 200 yds [+120] to Jawbone Overlook, with a view east to Duncan Knob across Crisman Hollow, and a long view southwest between Short and Kerns mountains. Charred stumps along this climb are the remains of a 10,000 acre forest fire in 1980.

The Jawbone Gap and Gap Creek trails provide an alternate 3.5 mi route to milepoint 42.8, passing a short spur trail to Duncan Knob.

Continue south along the ridge of Kerns Mountain [2450 to 2550]. The ridge is narrow and rocky at this end, wide and sandy at the south end. The trail at the north end alternates between short sections on the narrow ridge and longer sections along the slope on either side of the ridge. There are short, steep sections (sometimes switchbacked), to get between the ridge and the sideslope sections. One 200 ft section on the west slope passes along rock outcrops that are covered with leathery lichen and topped by dense mats of common polypody fern, green year-round (photo on next page). This ridge trail has almost continuous winter views through trees.

Camping is impossible on the northern half of this trail section. However, the flatter southern half of this section has potential tentsites and two small campsites within a half mile of Crisman Hollow Rd.

36.8 Crisman Hollow Rd, FR274, on a high saddle between Kerns and Waterfall mountains. [2330] Cache. Cross FR274, gentle ascent to ridge through old clearings.

37.0   Bear left along the ridge of Waterfall Mountain [2400]. Pass an overlook to the east with a view around the south end of Strickler Knob to the Blue Ridge. Dense fields of blueberry bushes. Watch for bears when berries are ripe.

37.4   Sharp turn right, descend [-900] on steps and steep switchbacks.

38.0   Massanutten Connector Tr, white-blazed, right. [1500] Bear left to enter the steep-sided drainage of Big Run.

38.2   Two-tent campsite along Big Run, reliable [1700]. Begin gradual ascent [+800]. Cross the run, ascend and bear left onto an old roadbed. Cross Big Run twice more, and ascend a steep, rocky section of tread before the drainage broadens and flattens.

40.1   Scothorn Gap Tr, yellow-blazed [2500], on a saddle between Middle and Waterfall Mountains. The Scothorn Gap and Gap Creek trails provide an alternate 2.6 mile route to milepoint 42.8, passing a short spur trail to Duncan Knob.

For camping, turn left onto Scothorn: an unreliable spring at 120 yds and campsites in old clearings at 500, 600, and 630 yds, plus potential tentsites.

The MT turns right at this trail intersection, and angles up the west face of Middle Mountain.

41.0   Cross the ridge of Middle Mountain. [2720] Angle down [-850] on east slope of Middle Mountain into Duncan

Common polypody fern (by Wil Kohlbrenner)

Hollow, between Middle and Massanutten mountains, eventually joining an old road in the hollow.

42.8 Gap Creek Tr, blue-blazed, left. [1870] An unblazed trail right, △, crosses reliable creek to a unique campsite, then continues to private property.

The MT continues on an old wagon road.

42.9 Two crossings of reliable creek.

43.2 Unique campsite right, △, at edge of reliable creek. *From October to May this is last reliable water for ~19 miles.*

45.5 Large campsite right, but unreliable creek.

45.8 Multi-tent campsite right, unreliable creek nearby. Bear right off roadbed onto trail, to avoid going onto private property.

45.9 Cross unreliable creek [1300]. Gentle ascent as the MT crosses shale barrens on the west slope of Massanutten Mountain. A wooden bridge at one point.

46.0 Old road crosses, with campsite left in a flat area.

46.1 SR675. [1300] The Camp Roosevelt picnic area is 120 yds left on SR675. Follow an unblazed path right off SR675 into the picnic area, trash bins, restrooms and water May to October. *Last reliable water for ~16 miles.* Cache in winter.

Cross SR675, ascend road toward a parking lot.

46.2 Right turn near Forest Service storage shed. Stephens Tr, yellow-blazed, goes straight across parking lot. The Stephens Tr provides an alternate route to milepoint 50.3.

The MT climbs Massanutten Mountain [+550] on switchbacks. There is a pit mine at mid-point. A deep V-cut in the upslope on the right leads to the bottom of the pit.

47.0 Edith Gap, SR675 again. [1850] View across the Shenandoah South Fork to Shenandoah National Park along the Blue Ridge. This is a hang glider launch site when winds are favorable. Cache.

Stay left along SR675, then turn left to continue north on a wide ridge road that is open to 4WD vehicles. Vehicle campsites along trail.

48.6 Bear left onto narrower trail. At a sharp switchback left, a well-worn unblazed trail leads to the base of an old microwave tower on the east slope of Kennedy Peak. No campsites, tentsites, water, or views. The MT curves around Kennedy Peak on its west slope.

49.3 An unblazed loop trail, left, for 100 yds, has a limited view of Fort Valley.

49.4 Kennedy Peak Tr, white-blazed, right [2380], [+220] to peak. If the sign is missing, you can miss the trail, since it joins at a shallow angle. The stone base of an old fire tower on the peak has a wooden floor and a wooden deck above, enclosing a mini-shelter (for one or two) on the highest point along the east ridge. No additional space for tents, however.

The MT continues north on ridge.

50.2 Ridge is flat, with campsite and potential tentsites right.

50.3 Stephens Tr, yellow-blazed, left. [2150] Begin many miles of saw-tooth ridge [1900 to 2100].

53.0 Habron Gap Tr, blue-blazed, right. [1930] Campsite 0.2 mi [-120] down Habron Gap Tr. Cache. The unblazed wagon road left descends to private property.

Ridge ahead is narrow, with excellent views of the South Fork of the Shenandoah to the east, Fort Valley to the west. Rocky tread.

56.5 Indian Grave Ridge Tr, purple-blazed, right. [1980]

56.6 Unblazed wagon road left descends to private property.

57.6 Multi-tent campsite, right [1840].

57.9 Milford Gap Tr, white-blazed, right only. [1760] The unblazed road left descends to private property and should not be used. Small campsite right.

58.4 The MT bears right off the ridge onto a narrow footpath called the Billy Goat section. Good views east. An unblazed trail rises along the ridge, but on the edge of private property.

59.0 The MT returns to the ridge.

61.3 Large campsite. [1800]

61.4 Tuscarora Tr, Veach Gap section, blue-blazed, joins from the right. [1780] Orange and blue blazes. This portion of the Tuscarora Tr follows Morgan's Rd, built by Daniel Morgan under orders from George Washington, who was anticipating the possible use of Fort Valley as a winter encampment for the Continental Army. Take a short walk to the right down the Tuscarora to develop an appreciation of this 240-year-old, very well-built road cut into the side of the mountain.

A bushwhack straight ahead on the ridge for 1.5 miles will rejoin the MT at 64.6.

Bear left to begin descent [-600] on Morgan's Rd.

62.3   Little Crease Shelter, right. Reliable spring. The shelter and nearby tentsites are busy on weekends.

62.4   Veach Gap Tr, yellow-blazed, left [1180], follows Morgan's Rd into Fort Valley. Begin ascent [+900] in the hollow between Little Crease and Massanutten mountains. Switchbacks near the end.

62.9   Campsite on unblazed path, △, right.

64.6   Ridge. [2080] Bear left along twisting ridge where Little Crease and Massanutten mountains meet.

65.4   Start steep descent of 300 ft.

65.7   Sherman Gap. [1960] Sherman Gap Tr joins from the right. Pink blazes of the Sherman Gap Tr join the orange and blue blazes of Massanutten and Tuscarora trails! Steep ascent.

65.8   Sherman Gap Tr, pink-blazed, leaves to the left. The Sherman Gap and Botts trails provide an alternate route to the picnic area road near milepoint 70.2. MT continues on ridge.

67.7   High point of ridge [1980]. Rocky, narrow trail ahead. Stone "steps."

68.1   Shawl Gap. [1710] Shawl Gap Tr, yellow-blazed, right. Buzzard Rock Tr, white-blazed, straight ahead. A 2-tent campsite, right. Potential tentsites along the Buzzard Rock Tr, then a unique campsite on a knob in 0.4 mi.

The Massanutten and Tuscarora trails turn left to begin descent [-970] into Fort Valley on switchbacks. Awkward footing on rocks.

68.2   Cross old wagon road. An unreliable rock-lined spring at this intersection. Some short flights of stone steps ahead.

69.4   At a bend right, a short unblazed trail goes left to a winter view of Fort Valley.

69.6   Cross old wagon road.

70.0   Switchback at edge of old wagon road. Small campsite 20 yds down the road bed. *You are entering the Passage Creek Day Use area where camping is prohibited except in the developed campgrounds.* Come onto gentle grades near Passage Creek, as trail bears left to parallel the creek.

70.1   Ruins of Elizabeth Furnace. Pig Iron and Charcoal interpretive trails begin here, to the left.

70.2   East end of a concrete bridge across Passage Creek. [740] Fifty yds *left* on the paved road there are restrooms and piped water (May to October) in the picnic area, no camping. The water in Passage Creek is not recommended, since it has flowed past many miles of home and pasture drainage, and under numerous road crossings.

Cross the bridge toward outer parking area, then turn left on a short blazed path.

70.3   Fort Valley Rd, SR678. There is a hand pump for water, year-round, in the Elizabeth Furnace Family Campground, 0.4 mi south along the left shoulder of SR678. Cross SR678, ascend [+170] on an eroded ore road along shale barren. Watch for pieces of furnace slag used to surface the road in the 1800s.

70.5   T-intersection [900]. You are outside the Passage Creek Day Use Area, and camping is permitted. The Bear Wallow section of the Tuscarora Tr, blue-blazed, turns left, with a large campsite 70 yds along Tuscarora. The Tuscarora and Meneka Peak trails provide an alternate route to milepoint 3.4.

The MT turns right to continue north on a wagon road parallel to Fort Valley Rd.

70.8   An unblazed trail leads right to cross SR678 and enter the Elizabeth Furnace Group Campground.

70.9   An unblazed trail leads right for 50 yds, to the south end of the Signal Knob Parking area. The MT runs parallel to the parking lot, so stay on the blazed trail if hiking through.

71.0   Cross a gravel road (right turn to the parking lot).

71.1   End of circuit at wooden bridge at the north end of the parking lot. [740]

4. Elizabeth Furnace – Signal Knob Group

ELIZABETH FURNACE Recreation Area, along Fort Valley Rd, provides a picnic area, a group camping area (by reservation only), and a family camping area. Two interpretive trails near the ruins of the Elizabeth Furnace explain the process of charcoal making and pig iron making, see Interpretive Trails. Other trails pass pit mines, trench mines, and charcoal hearths.

The north end of the 71-mile long Massanutten Trail crosses the area on an east-west path. Other long trails, including the Tuscarora Trail, provide alternate east-west paths. Short trails act as connectors between these long trails and provide a variety of circuit hikes.

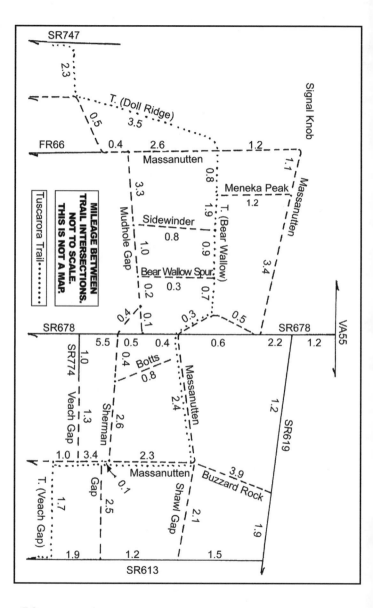

Bear Wallow Spur Trail

Difficulty: Elevation change 100 ft.
Length: 0.3 mi.   *Blazes:* White, dotted-i.
Maps: PATC G (F, 4) and TI 792.
Approach: From other trails.

This short north-south trail connects the Mudhole Gap Tr to the Tuscarora Tr.

North **South**   ·

0.0   **0.3**   Mudhole Gap Tr, purple-blazed. Northbound, follow old wagon road.

0.1   **0.2**   Northbound, bear right off wagon road.

Pass through a large oval area defined by a low stone wall. Stones may have been piled along a wooden fence to keep pigs(?) from digging under the fence. Cross a charcoal hearth, just north of this stone wall.

0.3   **0.0**   Tuscarora Tr-Bear Wallow section, blue-blazed. Southbound, gentle descent.

Botts Trail

Difficulty: Elevation change 100 ft.
Length: 0.8 mi.   *Blazes:* White, dotted-i.
Maps: PATC G (G, 4-5) and TI 792.
Approach: Fort Valley Rd.
Parking: Elizabeth Furnace Picnic Area. Note closing time for gate at bridge!

This north-south trail connects the Sherman Gap Tr to the Elizabeth Furnace Picnic Area along the east of Passage Creek, which saves fording the creek on the Sherman Gap Tr. The trail is in the Passage Creek Day Use Area, and is therefore closed to camping, except at the Elizabeth Furnace Campground.

South **North**

0.0   **0.8**   Picnic area *inner* parking lot, southeast corner. Southbound, follow occasional white blazes along wide grassy paths between picnic sites.

0.1   **0.7**   Edge of Passage Creek.

A narrow woods trail, rocky, brushy and muddy. Unblazed trails lead down to the creek, and the creek can generally be glimpsed (and heard) through the understory. There may be beaver activity in the creek.

0.8   0.0   Sherman Gap Tr, pink-blazed. A stone marker commemorates R. Wayne Botts, horseman and trail builder.

Buzzard Rock Trail

Difficulty: Elevation change 1300 ft, steep, loose tread.
Length: 3.9 mi.   *Blazes:* White, dotted-i.
Maps: PATC G (G-H, 2-4) and TI 792.
Approach: Waterlick - Bentonville.
Parking: Parking lot (8), west of SR619.

This north-south trail rises from SR619 and goes south along the saw-tooth ridge of Massanutten Mountain, passing Buzzard Rock, where you can look almost straight down into the gorge of Passage Creek as it exits from Fort Valley. Buzzards may be flying below you! The trail ends in Shawl Gap where it intersects the Massanutten, Tuscarora, and Shawl Gap trails.

This is a rugged trail. For about two miles, you will be stepping up and down on rocks and squeezing between them, with narrow footing above very steep slopes. If you experience vertigo, avoid this trail.

South   North

0.0   3.9   SR619. [690] Southbound, follow woods trail through a narrow section of the national forest. Follow blazes carefully to avoid trespassing on nearby private property, then begin a gradual ascent to the north.

1.8   2.1   On the north end of the ridge of Massanutten Mountain [1200], overlooking the ponds of the Fish Cultural Station. Southbound, continue ascending on the ridge. Northbound, turn south and descend on a narrow sidehill trail.

Trail is on the narrow, rocky ridge of the mountain.

2.3   1.6   Buzzard Rock. [1350] A long section of sharply tilted rocks forms the ridge. By squeezing past them and peering over them, you can look down 700 ft into Passage Creek gorge. Across the gorge is the Buzzard Rock Overlook on the Massanutten Tr.

Narrow trail, on the ridge of the mountain. Steep ascents and descents as the trail crosses peaks and sags along the ridge. Two campsites (1-tent, 2-tent) in one of the sags.

3.5   0.4   Highest point. [2040] Southbound, the trail widens. Just south of this point there is a multi-tent campsite, west, with an unusual campfire ring.

Loose tread.

3.9   0.0   Shawl Gap. [1710] Campsite. Shawl Gap Tr, yellow-blazed, descends east. Massanutten Tr, orange-blazed (straight ahead CW 3.0, right CCW 68.1), and Tuscarora Tr, blue-blazed, go south along the ridge and also descend west to Elizabeth Furnace area. Northbound, begin ascent, wide trail; the ridge is wide and sandy here, with potential tentsites.

Meneka Peak Trail

Difficulty: Elevation change 270 ft, scrambles.
Length: 1.2 mi.   *Blazes:* White, dotted-i.
Maps: PATC G (E, 3) and TI 792.
Approach: From other trails.

This north-south trail connects the Massanutten Tr to the Tuscarora Tr. It runs along the ridge of Green Mountain, crossing the highest point, Meneka Peak, with limited views to the east. (Pronounced meh-NEE-kuh.)

This trail is sometimes used as a bailout by circuit hikers from the Elizabeth Furnace area who decide time or energy do not permit a full round trip to Signal Knob.

South   North

0.0   1.2   Massanutten Tr, orange-blazed, (right CW 67.7, left CCW 3.4). [2200] Southbound, gentle ascent.

0.3   0.9   Two short, steep block fields (scrambles).

0.4   0.8   Two small two-tent campsites, west side.

0.5   0.7   Highest point. [2360] View east across Fort Valley and on to the Blue Ridge. Southbound, descend gradually, rocky.

1.2   0.0   Tuscarora Tr, Bear Wallow section, blue-blazed. [2090] Northbound, gentle ascent, but rocky.

Mudhole Gap Trail

Difficulty: Elevation change 460 ft, loose tread, mudholes. Five crossings of Little Passage Creek, which may be difficult in times of high water.

Length: 4.6 mi.   *Blazes:* Purple, dotted-i.

Maps: PATC G (E-G, 4-6) and TI 792.

Approach: East end: Fort Valley Rd. West end: FR66.

Parking: East end: Along the forest road (10) that begins opposite Elizabeth Furnace Family Camp. West end: parking lot (10) off FR66 opposite north entrance to Powells Fort Camp.

This east-west trail begins on the forest road directly opposite the entrance to the Elizabeth Furnace Family Campground. The trail follows the forest road for 3.5 miles, then follows a short descent through woods to an old wagon road that ascends along Little Passage Creek through the gap. The trail ends by intersecting the Massanutten Tr. This is a popular mountain bike and equestrian route.

West   East

0.0   4.6   SR678. [800] Westbound, begin gentle ascent on forest road. Bear right at two forks in the road. (The two left forks form a loop, with a half dozen hunter campsites.)

0.15   4.45   Sherman Gap Tr, pink-blazed, south, near a gate on the forest road.

0.3   4.3   Bear Wallow Spur Tr, white-blazed, north.

1.3   3.3   Sidewinder Tr, pink-blazed, north [1060]. An unblazed trail, south, leads to PATC's Glass House, on private property.

2.4   2.2   High point on forest road. [1260]

3.5   1.1   Westbound, leave the forest road at a turn around area, descend. Eastbound, join forest road.

3.6　1.0　Westbound, turn right on a wide wagon road. Eastbound, turn left and ascend on steep, narrowing tread.

Wagon road passes through a water gap in Green Mountain, a pine and hemlock gorge. Cross Little Passage Creek five times [lowest, 1100]. Mudholes in wet weather.

4.6　0.0　Massanutten Tr, orange-blazed (right CW 62.5, left CCW 8.6), running on FR66. [1200] Across FR66 is Powells Fort Camp, closed, used only for special events, no camping. Reliable piped spring just north of this point before a gate on FR66. Camping is not recommended anywhere along this driveable part of FR66.

Shawl Gap Trail

Difficulty:　Elevation change 1010 ft, steep.
Length:　2.1 mi.　　　　*Blazes:*　Yellow, dotted-i.
Maps:　PATC G (H-I, 4-5) and TI 792.
Approach:　Waterlick – Bentonville.
Parking:　(6) in a loop of driveway-like forest road off SR613, near mailbox 4900.

This east-west trail ascends from a parking area on the east side of Massanutten Mountain to Shawl Gap on the ridge, where it meets the Massanutten and Tuscarora trails at a common intersection with the Buzzard Rock Tr.

West　East
0.0　2.1　SR613. [700] Westbound, follow forest road past gate.

The road crosses overgrown fields, and dense sections of regrowth following old clearcutting and more recent clearcutting. Few trees available for blazes.

1.3　0.8　Westbound, enter open woods on a footpath.
1.9　0.2　Westbound, turn left on an old wagon road, steep. The descending road leads to private property. Eastbound hikers should be alert to a right turn here off the wagon road.
2.0　0.1　Trail turns at a small pond.

2.1 0.0 Massanutten Tr, orange-blazed (left CW 3.0, straight ahead CCW 68.1), also Tuscarora Tr, blue-blazed. [1710] The Buzzard Rock Tr, white-blazed, also enters this intersection from the north. Eastbound, begin steep descent on an old roadbed that once carried pig iron out of Fort Valley to barges on the South Fork of the Shenandoah River.

Sherman Gap Trail

Difficulty: Elevation change 1400 ft, steep, must ford Passage Creek.

Length: 5.9 mi. *Blazes:* Pink.

Maps: PATC G (F-H, 4-6) and TI 792.

Approach: Fort Valley Rd, Waterlick - Bentonville.

Parking: West end: (2) along Mudhole Gap Tr's forest road, and (60) in parking lot on Fort Valley Rd. East end: (2) in weeds along SR613, near private property.

This east-west trail begins at its west end near a locked gate on the forest road portion of the Mudhole Gap Tr. It goes south to a large horse trailer parking lot on Fort Valley Rd, then crosses the road, crosses Passage Creek, and climbs the west face of Massanutten Mountain, then descends the east face to SR613. In places, the surface may be poorly maintained for hiking.

Passage Creek must be waded – an easy process with normal water levels, but wading tends to restrict the trail's use to warmer weather.

East West

0.0 5.9 Mudhole Gap Tr, purple-blazed, near a locked gate on a forest road. [820] Eastbound, hike short woods path south, then bear left on old wagon road.

0.1 5.8 Westbound, take left fork on wagon road, since the right fork goes to a campsite.

Cross two small, deeply cut streambeds, unreliable.

0.4   5.5   Fort Valley Rd, SR678. Westbound, bear right off parking area's driveway, onto a woods trail that joins an old wagon road. Eastbound, cross SR678.

This is the flood plain of Passage Creek, muddy, with lush growth in summer.

0.5   5.4   Passage Creek. [760] The ford is wide, flat, gravel-bottomed. (The creek is reliable, but the water is not recommended, since it is the drainage for all of Fort Valley's farms, homes, road crossings, etc.) Eastbound, begin ascent out of the flood plain.

0.8   5.1   Botts Tr, white-blazed, north. [800] Stone memorial marker. Eastbound, ascend, angling south along the west face of the mountain. Westbound, descend into flood plain.

Cross four deeply cut streambeds, unreliable. Loss of canopy due to storm damage may result in heavy growth of brush.

3.0   2.9   Eastbound, bear left. Westbound, bear right, gentler grades ahead along the west flank of the mountain.

Very steep tread, on the fall line of the slope.

3.4   2.5   Massanutten Tr, orange-blazed (south CW 5.3, north CCW 65.8), and Tuscarora Tr, blue-blazed, on the ridge. [1980] Eastbound, turn right to run concurrent with other trails. Westbound, turn left, descend.

Orange, pink, and blue blazes! Steep.

3.5   2.4   Massanutten Tr, orange-blazed (south CW 5.4, north CCW 65.7), also Tuscarora Tr, blue-blazed, on the ridge. This low point is Sherman Gap. [1940] Westbound, turn right to run concurrent with other trails. Eastbound, turn left, descend east face of the mountain on switchbacks.

4.5   1.4   Eastbound, join old wagon road.

Tread alternates between eroding wheel tracks.

5.9   0.0   SR613. [580] Westbound, ascend on eroded roadbed next to private property.

Sidewinder Trail

Difficulty: Elevation change 140 ft.

Length: 0.8 mi.   *Blazes:* Pink, dotted-i.

Maps: PATC G (F, 4-5) and TI 792.

Approach: From other trails.

This north-south trail connects the Mudhole Gap Tr to the Tuscarora Tr, crossing two deep drainage areas.

North   South

0.0   0.8   Mudhole Gap Tr, purple-blazed, on forest road. [1060] Northbound, ascend short steep bank to a level wagon road.

0.1   0.7   Northbound, swing left off the wagon road, cross ravine and unreliable stream.

Trail is in open woods, good canopy.

0.5   0.3   Cross ravine and unreliable stream.

0.8   0.0   Tuscarora Tr, Bear Wallow section, blue-blazed. [1140] Southbound, descend.

Tuscarora Trail

Difficulty: Steep, loose tread.

Length: 20.9 mi.   *Blazes:* Tuscarora blue.

Maps: PATC G (A-K, 4-11) and TI 792.

Approach: West end: see below. Center: Fort Valley Rd. East end: Waterlick - Bentonville.

Parking: West end: along SR747. Center: Elizabeth Furnace Picnic Area outer parking lot (12). East end, parking area off SR613 (6) at trailhead.

The Tuscarora Trail crosses the north end of the Massanutten on its way between the north and south forks of the Shenandoah River. Going south, the trail enters the national forest on the west side of the Massanutten, after crossing the valley of the North Fork on private property and county parkland and roads. The Doll Ridge section of the trail climbs to the ridge of Three Top Mountain, briefly joins the Massanutten Tr, then goes north along the ridge of the mountain and descends to Little Passage Creek in Little Fort Valley.

The Bear Wallow section then climbs to the ridge of Green Mountain and descends gradually into Fort Valley. The trail then joins the tread of the Massanutten Tr to cross Fort Valley Rd at the Elizabeth Furnace Picnic Ground.

The trail continues to share the tread of the Massanutten Tr, climbing to Shawl Gap on the ridge of Massanutten Mountain and turning south to pass the Little Crease Shelter in Veach Gap. The Veach Gap section of the Tuscarora then leaves the Massanutten Tr, turning east to descend out of the national forest. The trail continues across the valley of the South Fork of the Shenandoah on the way to its trailhead on the Appalachian Trail in Shenandoah National Park.

Three sections of the trail are described here using earlier trail names, but signs along the trail refer only to the name, Tuscarora Tr. The southern half of this 250-mile trail was once called the Big Blue Trail, and old-timers remember that name with fondness.

Those who are backpacking the Tuscarora should use *A Guide to the Tuscarora Trail*, which supplies detailed descriptions of the trail in both directions, including portions of the trail on county roads, parkland, and private property.

This description is for hikers who want to hike a portion of the trail, perhaps including it in a circuit hike with other trails in the Elizabeth Furnace Group.

Tuscarora Trail, Doll Ridge Section

Vehicle approach to the western trailhead is from I-81, by two numbered routes, SR651 and SR747, but there are many turns.

Driving directions to the west trailhead.

0.0   Leave I-81 at exit 291, Toms Brook. Turn east on SR651, Mt Olive Rd.

1.0   Turn right, south, on US11 (and SR651).

1.2   Turn left off US11 on Hahns Lane, still SR651.

2.2   Turn right on Tea Berry Rd (SR651 and SR650). Road becomes gravel surfaced and narrow.

2.3   Turn left on Johnson Rd, SR651. (SR650 goes straight.)

3.1　　T-junction, turn right on SR747, Riverview Drive.

3.8　　At a sharp bend to the right (mailbox 1428), you have reached the trail. Note blue blazes along road. Find parking along the road in next quarter mile. Hike back to the sharp bend. Toms Brook runs parallel to the road.

The trail enters private property, a farm. The first 0.8 mi eastbound is along and across fields where cattle graze. If you bring a dog with you, the cattle may strongly challenge your right to be here. It's best to leave the dog at home when hiking this end of the trail.

East　**West**

0.0　**20.9**　SR747. [600] Eastbound, at a bend in the paved road, there are two driveways. Take left driveway, cross concrete cattle grate. Follow driveway past barn and descend toward river. CAUTION: Single wire fences strung on plastic insulators may be electrified.

0.1　**20.8**　Cross a long low-water bridge over the North Fork of the Shenandoah River. [550] Continue on driveway.

0.2　**20.7**　Eastbound, bear right away from the river on driveway; fields on both sides.

0.5　**20.4**　Eastbound, follow driveway left of a barn to the edge of a fenced yard for a farm house. Turn right at the fence, and follow a narrow farm lane, grassy surface. Lane curves left, is eroded, with fenced fields on both sides.

0.6　**20.3**　Eastbound, lane ends. Go through the left of two gates. *If you open any gate, be sure to close it securely.*

Cross pasture, along fence.

0.8　**20.1**　Go through gate. *If you open any gate, be sure to close it securely.* Eastbound, enter woods, and turn left to walk parallel to the fence.

You are on private property. The owner's use of these woods may produce misleading "trails," so remain on the blazed path.

0.9　**20.0**　Eastbound, bear left at a fork in the woods road.

Cross two drainage areas. Occasionally steep.

1.7　**19.2**　Eastbound, begin laurel thicket, where canopy

64　*Elizabeth Furnace–Signal Knob Group*

thins. Westbound, enter open woods under full canopy.

Eleven switchbacks. Tread is steep, gutted, with many loose rocks. Footing is hazardous when the tread is hidden under leaves or snow.

1.9   19.0   Sign that faces descending traffic marks approximate boundary of national forest. Silver "blazes" in this area are "no hunting" signals for hunters who are descending.

2.2   18.7   Ridge of Three Top Mountain. [1790] View. Descend.

Steep, one switchback.

2.3   18.6   Massanutten Tr, orange-blazed. The trails are concurrent for 35 yds. (Campsite 0.8 mi south on the Massanutten Tr.) Eastbound on Tuscarora, turn left and angle upslope toward ridge when Massanutten Tr starts to descend as CW 61.6. Westbound, straight ahead when Massanutten Tr turns south as CCW 9.5.

2.5   18.4   Ridge of Three Top Mountain. Westbound, begin angled descent on east slope of mountain.

Trail winds along ridge. [~1730] Rocky. Views to west.

5.3   15.6   Ridge of Three Top Mountain. Eastbound, descend on east slope of mountain.

5.8   15.1   Massanutten Tr on forest road, orange-blazed (north CW 65.4, south CCW 5.7). [1560] Eastbound, cross road, continue on Bear Wallow section below. Westbound, begin angled ascent of Three Top Mountain.

Tuscarora Trail, Bear Wallow Section

5.8   15.1   Massanutten Tr on FR66, orange-blazed (north CW 65.4, south CCW 5.7). [1560] Campsites 0.8 mi north on FR66. Westbound, cross road, continue on Doll Ridge section above. Eastbound, cross Little Passage Creek, reliable.

50 yds east of the Massanutten Tr, △, an unblazed path leads north 100 yds to a large campsite.

Steep switchbacks, loose tread.

6.6   14.3   Meneka Peak Tr, white-blazed, north, on the ridge of Green Mountain. [2090] A tiny campsite 10 yds south, then 10 yds west of the trail intersection. Descend, both directions.

8.1   **12.8**   Large campsite on a charcoal hearth, north.

8.5   **12.4**   Sidewinder Tr, pink-blazed, south. [1140] Unreliable stream just east of this intersection.

9.4   **11.5**   Bear Wallow Spur Tr, white-blazed, south. Unreliable stream just east of this intersection.

9.9   **11.0**   Trench mines and pit mines on both sides of the trail. Traces of old wagon roads.

10.1   **10.8**   Massanutten Tr, orange-blazed (south CW 0.6, north CCW 70.5). [900] Campsite on Tuscarora 50 yds west of this intersection. Westbound, turn left on the Bear Wallow section of the Tuscarora Tr, blue blazes only. Eastbound, turn right, sharing CW tread of Massanutten Tr, orange and blue blazes.

Eastbound, use the Massanutten Tr's clockwise description for trail details, starting at CW 0.6, going 9.1 miles, as far as CW 9.7.

Tuscarora Trail, Veach Gap Section

19.2   **1.7**   Massanutten Tr, orange-blazed (south CW 9.7, north CCW 61.4), on ridge of Massanutten Mountain. [1790]

Westbound, turn right along ridge sharing tread of the Massanutten Tr, orange and blue blazes. Use the Massanutten Tr counterclockwise description for details, starting at CCW 61.4, going 9.1 miles, as far as CCW 70.5, then continue above in the Tuscarora Trail Bear Wallow section.

Eastbound, turn left, leaving the ridge, blue blazes only. Loose tread. This is Morgan's Rd, built in the 1770s by Daniel Morgan, army engineer, under orders of George Washington. Note the excellent rock cribbing that supports this old roadbed and the road's uniform grade.

19.4   **1.5**   Westbound, turn right on old road, ascending. Eastbound, leave road on narrower tread.

Switchbacks, steep.

20.9 **0.0** Parking area off SR613. [830] Eastbound, follow blazes on driveway to SR613, turn right. Westbound, pass gate, descend briefly, then ascend [+960] to ridge.

Veach Gap Trail

Difficulty: Elevation change 200 ft, slippery footing in creekbed.
Length: 1.2 mi. *Blazes:* Yellow, dotted-i.
Maps: PATC G (G-H, 8) and TI 792.
Approach: Fort Valley Rd and SR774.
Parking: Parking lot (8) beyond the end of SR774, using a right-of-way over private land. Please respect landowner's rights and remain on the road.

This east-west trail connects to the Massanutten and Tuscarora trails by following an old crossing of Massanutten Mountain on Morgan's Rd, constructed under orders from General Washington to provide access to Fort Valley in case the Continental Army had to retreat. (The Sherman Gap Tr claims the same distinction!) The Tuscarora Tr, Veach Gap section, completes the east end of Morgan's Rd.

East **West**

0.0 **1.2** Parking area. [990] Eastbound, follow wagon road.

0.6 **0.6** Cross Mill Run, on old wagon road.

The wagon road is often in the bed of the run, on slippery rocks. This is Veach Gap, a water gap in Little Crease Mountain.

1.2 **0.0** Massanutten Tr, orange-blazed (right, CW 8.7, left CCW 62.4), also Tuscarora Tr, blue-blazed. [1190] Eastbound, turn right to reach Little Crease Shelter, and to continue on Morgan's Rd. Westbound, descend along wagon road parallel to Mill Run.

Campground – Picnic Area Circuit

Difficulty: Elevation change 300 ft. Loose tread. *Passage Creek must be crossed, which is difficult when water is high.*

Length: 3.4 mi.

Maps: PATC G (F-G, 4) and TI 792.

Approach: Fort Valley Rd.

Parking: Across Fort Valley Rd from Elizabeth Furnace Family Campground.

This is a pleasant summer hike in the woods on both sides of Passage Creek in the Elizabeth Furnace Recreation Area, with no steep ascents and minimum elevation gain. The terrain is mostly shaded and often wet. The hike passes through areas that saw intense mining activity when the furnace was in production.

The circuit utilizes five trails. The clockwise route described here has two short, steep descents, but all ascents are gradual.

The circuit begins and ends at the start of the Mudhole Gap Tr, on the forest road directly opposite the entrance to the Elizabeth Furnace Family Campground.

Miles

0.0   Fort Valley Rd. Hike west on the Mudhole Gap Tr, purple-blazed, on the forest road. Bear right at each fork in the road.

0.15   Pass Sherman Gap Tr, pink-blazed, left. Pass a gate across the road.

0.3   Bear Wallow Spur Tr, white-blazed, right. Turn right, on rocky wagon road, then bear right onto another old wagon road.

0.6   Tuscarora Tr, blue-blazed. Turn right, and cross a streambed. Pass pits and trenches from mining activity.

1.3   Massanutten Tr, orange-blazed. Turn right on orange and blue blazes. Descend on an eroded ore road across shale barren. Watch for glassy pieces of furnace slag that were used to surface the old roadbed.

1.6   Cross Fort Valley Rd, descend a short path and enter the outer parking lot for Picnic Area. Turn right on paved road, cross bridge, and *stay on unblazed paved road* to enter the inner parking lot.

1.8   At far left corner of the inner parking lot, find Botts Tr, white-blazed. Follow occasional white blazes on trees along wide, grassy paths between picnic sites.

1.9   Edge of Passage Creek at last picnic site. Follow narrow woods trail; rocky, brushy, and muddy. Gradual ascent. Passage Creek is on your right, and unblazed paths made by fishermen lead down to the creek. There may be beaver activity in the creek.

2.6   Sherman Gap Tr, pink-blazed. Stone marker nearby. Turn right, and descend toward Passage Creek.

2.9   Cross Passage Creek. The ford is wide, flat, gravel-bottomed. Continue on a brushy trail in the flood plain of the creek.

3.0   Cross Fort Valley Rd onto a gravel entrance to a large parking lot, then bear right off the entrance road onto a pink-blazed trail. This section of the Sherman Gap Trail swings north parallel to Fort Valley Rd, and crosses small feeder streams that flow toward Passage Creek. Pass campsites (that are not part of the Family Campground).

3.3   Mudhole Gap Tr, purple-blazed, on forest road. Turn right, follow blazes along the road.

3.4   Fort Valley Rd, end of circuit.

Picnic Area – East Ridge Circuit

Difficulty:	Elevation change 1100 ft, steep, rock steps.
Length:	8.0 mi, omitting side trip to Buzzard Rock.
	11.2 mi, including side trip to Buzzard Rock.
Maps:	PATC G (G-H, 4-6) and TI 792.
Approach:	Fort Valley Rd.
Parking:	Elizabeth Furnace Picnic Area, outer lot.

WARNING: The gate that blocks the road to the inner parking lot is closed and locked every evening. Be sure to park in the outer lot.

This circuit climbs to Shawl Gap on the ridge of Massanutten Mountain, goes south along the ridge on the Massanutten Trail, then returns on the Sherman Gap and Botts trails. The circuit passes the ruins of the Elizabeth Furnace, and the Charcoal and Pig Iron interpretive trails near the furnace. Views east from the ridge. An optional side trip to Buzzard Rock adds another 3.2 miles.

Miles

0.0   Picnic Area outer parking lot. Cross bridge from the outer parking lot, turn left, on orange and blue blazes of the Massanutten and Tuscarora trails. The trail follows the creek downstream then bears right, away from the creek.

0.1   Ruins of the Elizabeth Furnace, right. The Pig Iron and Charcoal trails start near the furnace. Begin ascent of the west face of Massanutten Mountain on switchbacks.

0.8   At a bend left, an unblazed trail goes straight ahead a short distance to a limited view of Fort Valley. The blazed trail becomes rocky, with flights of steps.

2.0   Trail crosses large, tipped rocks as it nears the gap.

2.1   Shawl Gap. [1710] Shawl Gap Tr, yellow-blazed, straight ahead. Buzzard Rock Trail, white-blazed, left. (Buzzard Rock is 1.6 miles north. Use the Buzzard Rock Trail description to add this optional side trip.) To continue the circuit, turn right on the Massanutten and Tuscarora trails, orange- and blue-blazed. Ascend on rocky, steep tread.

2.5   High point of the ridge [1980]. Rocky tread continues. Occasional views left across the South Fork of the Shenandoah River to the Blue Ridge.

3.6   Tread becomes less rocky.

4.4   Sherman Gap Tr, pink-blazed, joins from right. Turn right and descend, following pink blazes. Very steep.

4.8   Bear right, gentler grades ahead along the west flank of the mountain. Gradual descent, crossing four deeply cut streambeds. Heavy growth of brush in places where loss of the canopy due to storm damage lets sunlight reach the forest floor.

7.0 Botts Tr, white-blazed, right. Stone memorial nearby. Turn right, follow white blazes on gradual descent. Tread beomes rocky, brushy, and muddy. Passage Creek is on the left, with occasional unblazed trails to the creek made by fishermen.

7.7 Bear right, away from the creek onto a wide grassy strip that runs between picnic sites. Occasional white blazes lead to inner parking lot for the picnic area. Follow paved road from the inner parking lot, unblazed.

8.0 End of circuit at bridge over Passage Creek.

Signal Knob Circuits

Difficulty: Elevation change 2400 ft, steep, block fields, loose tread.

Length: 10.7 mi, from Signal Knob parking lot.

10.8 mi, from Elizabeth Furnace Group Camp.

11.3 mi, from Elizabeth Furnace Picnic Area.

11.7 mi, from Elizabeth Furnace Family Camp.

Maps: PATC G (E-G, 2-5) and TI 792.

Approach: Fort Valley Rd.

Parking: Signal Knob parking lot, or Picnic Area parking lot, or opposite the entrance to the Family Campground.

This is the most popular circuit hike on the Massanutten. This text describes a counterclockwise route beginning at the Signal Knob Parking area. The most difficult portion of the hike is the Massanutten Tr to Signal Knob, and many hikers prefer to tackle that while they are fresh.

To start from the Elizabeth Furnace Group Campground, cross Fort Valley Rd and follow the short unblazed trail to the orange-blazed Massanutten Tr. Turn right. You are then at 10.5 in the circuit description below.

To start from the Elizabeth Furnace picnic area parking lot, hike west on the Massanutten and Tuscarora trails, orange-and-blue blazed, crossing Fort Valley Rd and ascending along a steep trail on shale barren for 0.3 mi. You are then at 10.2 in the circuit description below.

To start from the Elizabeth Furnace Family Campground, cross Fort Valley Rd and follow the purple-blazed Mudhole Gap Tr west on the gravel road opposite the campground entrance. Bear right at forks in the road, and pass a gate. After 0.3 miles, turn right onto the white-blazed Bear Wallow Spur Tr, and follow it for 0.3 miles to the Tuscarora Tr, blue-blazed. Turn right. You are then at 9.4 in the circuit description below.

Miles

0.0   Begin the basic circuit at the north end of the Signal Knob Parking area. Hike north on the Massanutten Tr, orange-blazed. (Ignore yellow blazes.) Ascend on occasionally rocky tread.

0.2   A stone cabin (locked) above the trail is a Forest Service administrative building.

0.4   Sharp turn right at a spring in a ravine. As the trail continues to climb, there are occasional views right across Passage Creek.

1.5   Buzzard Rock Overlook. [1540] (Buzzard Rock is east across the gorge.) Bear left and follow orange blazes across block fields. Difficult footing.

2.2   Fort Valley Overlook left. [1800] Continue on block fields.

3.4   Meneka Peak Tr, white-blazed, left. [2200] (A left turn here leads in 1.2 miles to point 6.6 below. This produces a shorter circuit, but misses Signal Knob.) Continue the full circuit ascending on rocky tread across the north end of Green Mountain, then descend toward Signal Knob. Join a gravel road and pass the TV tower site, then bear right off the road onto a blazed trail to the knob.

4.5   Signal Knob. The view includes the north end of the Shenandoah Valley, Great North and Little North mountains to the west. Strasburg is at the foot of the knob, and the North Fork of the Shenandoah turns east here (hidden by trees) to be joined by Passage Creek and to eventually unite with the South Fork near Front Royal.

Continue the circuit by hiking south on the Massanutten Tr, orange-blazed. Join the gravel road for a steep descent into the valley between Green Mountain (left) and Three Top Mountain (right). Piles of finely ground limestone at the edge of a creek to the left of the road are dumped by the Forest Service to reduce stream acidity caused by acid rain.

5.8   Tuscarora Tr, blue-blazed, crosses. Turn left, and follow blue blazes. Cross Little Passage Creek. Begin ascent on steep switchbacks, loose tread.

6.6   Meneka Peak Tr, white-blazed, left, on the ridge of Green Mountain. [2090] Descend on switchbacked tread on the east slope of Green Mountain.

8.1   Large campsite on a charcoal hearth, left.

8.5   Sidewinder Tr, pink-blazed, right. [1140] Cross streambed just east of this intersection.

9.4   Bear Wallow Spur Tr, white-blazed, right. (To return to the Family Campground, turn right at this point, follow white blazes, then turn left on the purple-blazed Mudhole Gap Tr.) Continue the circuit by crossing streambed.

10.2   Massanutten Tr, orange-blazed. (To return to the Elizabeth Furnace Picnic Area, turn right at this point and follow orange and blue blazes.) To continue the circuit, turn left, following orange blazes of the MT. This is an old wagon road which descends and runs parallel to Fort Valley Rd.

10.5   An unblazed trail, right. (To return to the Group Campground, turn right on this short trail.)

10.7   End of circuit at Signal Knob Parking area. Hikers who began at an alternate starting point should continue past this point, hiking north, using the circuit description from 0.0.

Campground – Reservoir Circuits

Difficulty: Elevation change 1600 ft short route, 1800 ft long route, loose tread, eight crossings of Little Passage Creek.

Length: 11.7 mi, omitting side trip to Signal Knob.

  14.5 mi, including side trip to Signal Knob.

Maps: PATC G (E-G, 2-4) and TI 792.

Approach: Fort Valley Rd.

Parking: Along forest road (10) opposite the entrance to the Elizabeth Furnace Family Campground.

The shorter circuit is made up of four trails. The longer circuit includes Signal Knob, and uses another trail. This text describes a clockwise route that leaves most of the steeper grades as downhill hiking near the end of the circuit.

Miles

0.0 Fort Valley Rd opposite the Elizabeth Furnace Family Campground. Hike west on the Mudhole Gap Tr, purple-blazed. [800] Gentle ascent on forest road. Bear right at two forks in the road.

0.15 Pass Sherman Gap Tr, pink-blazed, left, near a gate on the forest road. Continue past the gate.

0.3 Pass Bear Wallow Spur Tr, white-blazed, right.

1.3 Pass Sidewinder Tr, pink-blazed, right. [1060]

2.4 High point on the forest road. [1260]

3.5 Leave the forest road at a turn around area, descend.

3.6 Turn right on a wide wagon road which passes through a water gap in Green Mountain. Cross Little Passage Creek five times [lowest, 1100]. Mudholes during wet weather.

4.6 Massanutten Tr, orange-blazed, on FR66. [1200] Turn right. Pass piped spring, left. Pass locked gate.

5.8 Cross Little Passage Creek.

6.6 The blazed trail bears left off the road to pass the Strasburg Reservoir on its west side. (The road continues unblazed and passes the reservoir on its right shore. Both routes rejoin north of the reservoir.) *The reservoir is on private property and is not developed for public use.*

7.2   The blazed trail rejoins the forest road and both continue north toward Signal Knob.

7.5   Tuscarora Tr, blue-blazed, crosses. (For longer circuit see below.) Turn right onto Tuscarora Tr and cross Little Passage Creek. Begin ascent on switchbacks, rocky tread.

8.3   Meneka Peak Tr, white-blazed, left, on the ridge of Green Mountain. [2090] Continue east, descending on blue-blazed trail, switchbacks, occasionally rocky or wet.

9.8   Large campsite on a charcoal hearth, left.

10.2   Pass Sidewinder Tr, pink-blazed, right.

11.1   Bear Wallow Spur Tr, white-blazed, right. Turn right, and follow white blazes along old wagon roads.

11.4   Mudhole Gap Tr, purple-blazed. Turn left.

11.7   Fort Valley Rd, end of circuit.

Longer circuit, including Signal Knob

7.5   Tuscarora Tr, blue-blazed, crosses. Continue straight ahead on the road, following Massanutten Trail's orange blazes. Ascend on a road that gets steeper and seems endless!

8.6   At a bend in the road, follow the blazed trail left off the road.

8.7   Signal Knob. The view includes the north end of the Shenandoah Valley, Great North and Little North mountains to the west. Strasburg is at the foot of the knob, and the North Fork of the Shenandoah turns east here (hidden by trees) to be joined by Passage Creek and to eventually unite with the South Fork near Front Royal. Continue the circuit by hiking east on the orange-blazed Massanutten Trail which rejoins the road and passes a TV tower before entering sparse woods as a ridge trail. Gradually ascend and cross the rocky north end of Green Mountain, descending on the east slope.

9.9   Meneka Peak Tr, white-blazed. Turn right; gentle ascent.

10.2   Two short scrambles on block fields.

10.4   Highest point. [2360] Limited view east across Fort Valley to the Blue Ridge. Gradual descent, occasionally rocky.

11.1   Tuscarora Tr, blue-blazed. Turn left and resume at milepoint 8.3 in the shorter circuit.

Some Backpack Routes

Three backpack routes are described below. The individual trail descriptions and the mileage diagram for the Elizabeth Furnace Group provide the data required for planning a trip.

Circuit, 15.1 miles. From SR678, Elizabeth Furnace picnic area parking lot, go west on Massanutten Tr (CCW 70.2 to CCW 71.1, then CCW 0.0 to CCW 8.6), then east on Mudhole Gap Tr, north on Sidewinder Tr, and east on Tuscarora Tr-Bear Wallow section. Then return on Massanutten Tr (CW 0.6 to CW 0.9).

Point-to-point, 24.8 miles. From SR619, south on Buzzard Rock Tr, west on Massanutten Tr (CCW 68.1 to CCW 70.5), west on Tuscarora Tr-Bear Wallow section, north on Meneka Peak Tr, west on Massanutten Tr (CCW 3.4 to CCW 5.7), "west" on Tuscarora Tr-Doll Ridge section, northeast on Massanutten Tr (CW 61.6 to CW 65.4), east on Tuscarora Tr-Bear Wallow section, south on Bear Wallow Spur Tr, east on Mudhole Gap Tr to SR678.

Point-to-point, Tuscarora Tr, 21.2 miles. From SR613, west on Tuscarora Tr-Veach Gap section, north on Massanutten Tr (CCW 61.4 to CCW 70.5, still Tuscarora), west on Tuscarora Tr-Bear Wallow section, south and west on Tuscarora Tr-Doll Ridge section to SR747.

5. West Group

MASSANUTTEN Tr runs along western ridges from Signal Knob south to Kerns Mountain. This section describes the trails that intersect the Massanutten Tr between the Elizabeth Furnace group and the Crisman Hollow group.

The Peters Mill Run Tr (OHV, ATV) and FR374 run parallel to the Massanutten Trail at lower elevations, and the side trails that connect them provide circuit hike opportunities, with use of FR374 or the OHV trail.

7-Bar None Trail

Difficulty: Elevation change 200 ft.
Length: 0.5 mi.   *Blazes:* Blue, dotted-i.
Maps: PATC G (D, 14) and TI 792.
Approach: From other trails.

This east-west trail links the Massanutten Tr on the ridge of Powell Mountain to the Peters Mill Run Tr (OHV) in the long valley between Powell and Green Mountains.

East   **West**

0.0   **0.5**   Massanutten Tr (south CCW 17.5, north CW 53.6), orange-blazed. [1840] Eastbound, descend. Steep.

0.3   **0.2**   Cross Peters Mill Run. [1640] Tread is boggy after wet weather.

0.5   **0.0**   Peters Mill Run Tr (OHV), yellow-V-blazed. [1740] Westbound, descend.

Bear Trap Trail

Difficulty: Elevation change 200 ft.
Length: 0.4 mi.   *Blazes:* Pink, dotted-i.
Maps: PATC G (D, 17) and TI 792.
Approach: From other trails.

This east-west trail links the Massanutten Tr on the ridge of Powell Mountain to the Peters Mill Run Trail as it descends north, down the valley between Powell and Green Mountains.

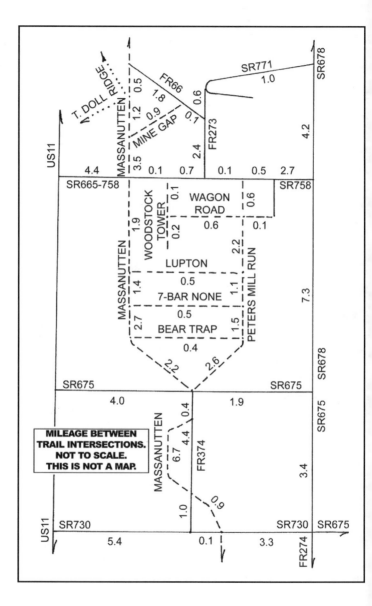

MILEAGE BETWEEN
TRAIL INTERSECTIONS.
NOT TO SCALE.
THIS IS NOT A MAP.

East   West

0.0   0.4   Massanutten Tr (south CCW 20.2, north CW 50.9), orange-blazed. [2360] Eastbound, descend.

Switchbacks.

0.2   0.2   Cross drainage area. [2160]

0.4   0.0   Peters Mill Run Tr (OHV), yellow-V-blazed. [2260] Westbound, descend.

Lupton Trail

Difficulty: Elevation change 290 ft.

Length: 0.5 mi.   *Blazes:* Purple, dotted-i.

Maps: PATC G (D, 13) and TI 792.

Approach: From other trails.

This east-west trail links the Massanutten Tr on the ridge of Powell Mountain to the Peters Mill Run Tr (OHV) in the valley between Powell and Green mountains.

East   West

0.0   0.5   Massanutten Tr (south CCW 16.1, north CW 55.0), orange-blazed. [1800] Eastbound, descend.

Steep, old wagon road.

0.4   0.1   Cross Peters Mill Run. [1460] Tread is boggy after wet weather.

0.5   0.0   Peters Mill Run Tr, OHV, yellow-V-blazed. [1510] Westbound, descend.

Mine Gap Trail

Difficulty: Elevation change 670 ft, steep.

Length: 0.9 mi.   *Blazes:* Purple, dotted-i.

Maps: PATC G (D-E, 8) and TI 792.

Approach: Powells Fort (FR273 – FR66).

Parking: Pull-off (6) from FR66, near trailhead.

This east-west trail links FR66 to the Massanutten Tr on the ridge of Three Top Mountain.

West   East

0.0   0.9   FR66. [1100] Ascend westbound.

Wide, grassy wagon road under canopy.

0.5   0.4   Westbound, start trail section built over four years by Woodstock Girl Scout Troop 284 as their Silver Project.

Switchback. Cross trench mine on upper section.

0.7   0.2   Westbound, sharp turn onto old wagon road. Eastbound, *watch carefully* for this turn off road, east.

Steep.

0.9   0.0   Massanutten Tr (south CCW 10.7, north CW 60.4), orange-blazed. [1770] There is a 2-tent campsite off the Massanutten Tr, 50 yds to the south. Eastbound, descend on wagon road.

Peters Mill Run Trail

The Peters Mill Run Tr is not fully described in this guide. It is a wide road for ATVs and OHVs, blazed with a yellow-V.

Climbing north from Edinburg Gap, it is on shale outcrops and hard-packed clay that is slippery when wet. As it drops into Little Fort Valley, it is on gravel and sandstone outcrops.

The trail is open to bike, horse, and foot traffic, and the motorized traffic is supposed to yield to others. As a hiker, the natural reaction is to step out of the roadbed – you will be rewarded by the roar of an engine, a cloud of dust in dry weather or splashing mud after wet weather. It usually has a lot of trash.

Avoid this trail on weekends and holidays.

Wagon Road Trail

Difficulty: Elevation change 550 ft, steep.
Length: 0.7 mi.   *Blazes:* White, dotted-i.
Maps: PATC G (D, 11) and TI 792.
Approach: Detrick – Woodstock.
Parking: In Little Fort Recreation Area (4), just past registration board.

This east-west trail follows a stagecoach road, used in the early 1800s to reach the Seven Fountains Resort in Fort Valley from the railroad in Woodstock. Coaches traveled the route seven times each day. There are weathered posts along both sides of the trail, sawed off at an angle, with a number incised in the slanted surface. Each post marks a station; each station was once described in a Forest Service brochure. You may want to speculate about what was being described. (Post #11 is below a charcoal hearth – black charcoal dust under the leaf mold.) Unfortunately, the old road surface is fast disappearing due to erosion.

West	East	
0.0	**0.7**	Little Fort Recreation Area. [1340] The trailhead is between campsites 8 and 9, near the privies.
0.1	**0.6**	Cross Peters Mill Run Tr (OHV), yellow-V-blazed.
		Switchbacks, steep.
0.7	**0.0**	Woodstock Tower Tr, pink-blazed, on the ridge.

[1890] An unblazed portion of the wagon road continues and descends to SR758 and parking areas where the Massanutten Tr (south CCW 14.2, north CW 56.9) crosses the road.

Woodstock Tower Trail

Difficulty:	Almost level, but a few large stone steps.
Length:	0.25 mi. *Blazes:* Pink, dotted-i.
Maps:	PATC G (D, 11) and TI 792.
Approach:	Detrick – Woodstock.
Parking:	Along SR758 (40).

This spur trail leads south along the ridge of Powell Mountain from SR758. The metal tower was built in 1935 by "CCC boys." See CGS marker in concrete base.

There is a hang-glider launch site along the Massanutten Tr, 0.25 miles west and south of the tower. When winds cooperate, the area swarms with hang-gliding enthusiasts with two or three colorful gliders floating gracefully along the ridge.

The view to the west includes the Seven Bends area of the North Fork of the Shenandoah River, Woodstock, vehicles moving along I-81 in the valley beyond it, and the border with

West Virginia along Great North Mountain on the horizon. Directly to the east is Milford Gap and beyond, on the horizon, is Shenandoah National Park on the Blue Ridge.

Note that SR758 is a dirt road that may be damaged by storms and winter weather. It may be closed by gates at each end until county road crews can regrade it. From Detrick, you can park at the Little Fort Recreation Area and ascend to the ridge on the Wagon Rd Tr. From Woodstock, the locked gate leaves you with a long, steep climb [+890] up the road.

South

0.0 SR758, top of ridge. [1890] The trailhead is next to a sign set in stone.

0.1 Wagon Rd Tr, white-blazed, east.

0.25 Woodstock Tower. An unblazed, unmaintained trail continues past the tower, turns west off the crest, and descends to the Massanutten Tr (south CCW 14.4, north CW 56.7) near the hang-glider site. If you take this route to talk to hang-glider enthusiasts, you can return north along the Massanutten Tr, orange-blazed, to SR758.

6. East Group

ALONG the ridge of the Massanutten the trail that bears its name runs from the Elizabeth Furnace Group on the north end to the Crisman Hollow Group on the south end. This section describes the side trails that make possible some loop hikes from Page Valley Rd (SR684) on the east face of the mountain or from SR675 near Camp Roosevelt on the west face.

Kennedy Peak and sawtooth ridge, looking east, from Jawbone Overlook (by Wil Kohlbrenner)

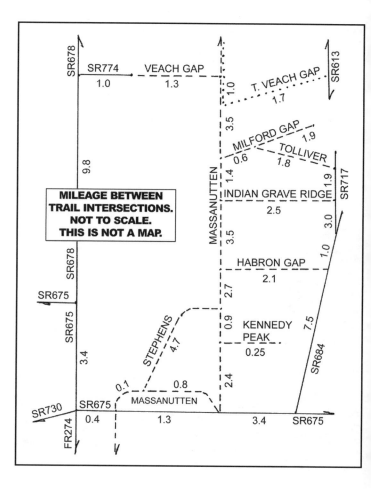

MILEAGE BETWEEN
TRAIL INTERSECTIONS.
NOT TO SCALE.
THIS IS NOT A MAP.

Habron Gap Trail

Difficulty: Elevation change 1230 ft, steep.
Length: 2.1 mi.   *Blazes:* Blue, dotted-i.
Maps: PATC G (H-I, 16) and TI 792.
Approach: Page Valley Rd.
Parking: Park at Public Boat Landing on SR684. This landing was historically called "Fosters Landing," but the name has not appeared on any sign for many years.

This east-west trail ascends the east face of Massanutten Mountain on tread that was relocated in 2002. The trailhead is now 20 yds north of the entrance to the parking area.

West   **East**
0.0   **2.1**   SR684. [700] Westbound, ascend in woods, crossing low finger ridges, trending north, then on steeper trail and an old road.
1.7   **0.4**   Panoramic views [1700] to the east across the South Fork, to the ridgeline in Shenandoah National Park. Westbound, swing left around the north face of a knob.
1.9   **0.2**   Campsite. [1810] Eastbound, swing right around the north face of a knob.
             Tread is on a steep old roadbed.
2.1   **0.0**   Massanutten Tr (north CCW 53.0, south CW 18.1), orange-blazed, in Habron Gap. [1930] Eastbound, descend.

Indian Grave Ridge Trail

Difficulty: Elevation change 1240 ft, steep, loose tread.
Length: 2.5 mi.   *Blazes:* Purple, dotted-i.
Maps: PATC G (H-J, 13) and TI 792.
Approach: Page Valley Rd.
Parking: In a lot just off of SR717 (6).

This east-west trail ascends the east face of Massanutten Mountain, following a wagon road that once crossed the mountain through a gap. The road climbs along a finger ridge which was reputed to hold the grave site of Native Americans.

All that is left of the grave is a ditch through several piles of rocks.

West	East	
0.0	2.5	Parking lot. [740] Westbound, descend at first, then ascend. Switchbacks, steep.
0.1	2.4	Primitive camping area.
1.0	1.5	Grave site to south in woods, no path. Westbound, just beyond grave site, turn right, small wildlife pond to right, begin steep ascent. The pond and turn mark the location of the grave site. The grave site is below the turn and south of the trail.
2.3	0.2	Westbound, enter a gap between a small knob on right and main ridge on left. Eastbound, steep descent. Switchbacks on steep, loose tread.
2.5	0.0	Massanutten Tr (north CCW 56.5, south CW 14.6), orange-blazed. [1980] Eastbound, descend.

Kennedy Peak Trail

Difficulty: Rise 220 ft.
Length: 0.25 mi.   *Blazes:* White, dotted-i.
Maps: PATC G (H, 19) and TI 792.
Approach: From Massanutten Tr.

Kennedy Peak is a popular destination for a day hike. The trailhead can be approached from the north or the south along the Massanutten Tr. Also, see circuit hike description.

The peak's name is derived from an earlier name, Canaday.

Miles

0.0   On the Massanutten Tr at CW 21.7, CCW 49.4. [2380] The trailhead can be missed if hiking north (CCW), because it is a sharp turn to the right off the Massanutten Tr *after hiking past the peak on its west face*. Begin ascent along the rocky ridge.

0.25   Kennedy Peak lookout, a wooden deck over the stone base of a former fire lookout tower. [2600] Excellent views.

Be careful on return to the Massanutten Tr. Hikers have unthinkingly turned the wrong way and become "lost."

Milford Gap Trail

Difficulty: Elevation change 1050 ft, steep, loose tread, hidden hazards.

Length: 2.5 mi. *Blazes:* White, dotted-i.

Maps: PATC G (H-J, 10-11) and TI 792.

Approach: From other trails.

This east-west trail connects Milford Gap, on the ridge, to the closed campsite at Hazard Mill, near the Shenandoah South Fork.

The trail uses a portion of an old stagecoach route over the mountain. This well-built mountain road has not been maintained and is now eroded down to bedrock in many places.

The old road to the west of the ridge crosses private property and has been discontinued as a trail. Please respect the property owner's rights: do not hike up or down the mountain on the west face.

The Hazard Mill Campground was closed when the Forest Service gave up a right-of-way over private property along the west bank of the river. Only the level tent pads remain along a grassy loop road in a beautiful grove of pines and hardwoods, perched on a finger ridge above the river. The restrooms are closed, and the water pump has been removed, but dispersed camping is allowed. Do not try to access this campsite from the north, along the gated, private road that parallels the river. The property owner enforces the NO TRESPASSING signs!

East   West

0.0   2.5   Milford Gap, on Massanutten Tr (north CCW 57.9, south CW 13.2), orange-blazed. [1750] Eastbound, descend; gutted roadbed.

The hiking surface is steep, and in many places is just a wide ribbon of rocks, some loose. There is one switchback at the midpoint of this section, and a large campsite 100 yds above the switchback. The upper half of this section is supported by impressive, high rock cribbing.

0.6   1.9   Tolliver Tr, orange-blazed, at a switchback. [1340] Tolliver Tr descends, southerly, along a stagecoach route. Milford Gap Tr descends, easterly, on gutted roadbed.

The hiking surface is often depressed in the middle, where seeps keep the tread wet and muddy. In mid-summer, lush grass grows in the thick mud, and the combination is slippery. In winter, it freezes.

2.2   0.3   Eastbound, right turn onto a wide trail, so be alert to blazes. Westbound, turn left and ascend.

2.3   0.2   Cross FR236, a wide grassy forest road. East-bound, continue descent. (Westbound, turn left onto FR236, for a short easy return to Tolliver trailhead parking.)

2.4   0.1   Cross drainage system. Eastbound, turn right to ascend and cross a finger ridge. Westbound, turn left to cross drainage and begin ascent.

2.5   0.0   Hazard Mill campground road. [700] East-bound, the camp center is to the right. Westbound from the campground, turn left off the campground road.

Stephens Trail

Difficulty: Elevation change 870 ft, steep.
Length: 4.7 mi.   *Blazes:* Yellow, dotted-i.
Maps: PATC G (G-H, 19-21) and TI 792.
Approach: Edinburg - Luray.
Parking: Parking lot off SR675, reached by following an 80-yard section of the Massanutten Tr along a gravel driveway.

This north-south trail follows the contour lines of the lower slopes of Massanutten Mountain, often on old woods roads, until it intersects a wagon road, then turns east to follow the wagon road to the ridge of Massanutten Mountain. The trail is named for a man who for many years manned the fire tower on Kennedy Peak and used the old wagon road to reach the ridge.

North   South

0.0   4.7   Parking lot on the Massanutten Tr (north CCW 46.2, south CW 24.9), orange-blazed. [1320] Stephens Tr begins near a brown Forest Service shed, crosses the parking lot and descends into woods, on yellow blazes. Southbound, cross parking lot to join Massanutten Tr on entrance driveway.

Trail rises and falls, going in and out of drainage areas. Tread may be muddy after heavy rains.

3.8   **0.9**   Cross a wagon road. Northbound, ascend.

3.9   **0.8**   Northbound, turn left on wagon road. Southbound, turn right off road.

Switchbacks. Steep.

4.7   **0.0**   Massanutten Tr (north CCW 50.3, south CW 20.8), orange-blazed. [2150] There is a view of Page County 50 yds east of this point, where an unblazed trail descends to private property.

Tolliver Trail

Difficulty: Rise 600 ft, steep.
Length: 1.8 mi.   *Blazes:*   Orange, dotted-i.
Maps: PATC G (I-J, 11-12) and TI 792.
Approach: Page Valley Rd.
Parking: At turnaround area on FR236, off SR 717.

This trail provides access to the Milford Gap Tr and to the abandoned campground at Hazard Mill.

Miles

0.0   Trail leaves the turnaround area [740] on a wide grassy roadbed, passing old gate posts, then a gate at a turn. This gate, known as "236 Hazard Mill, 1st gate" is opened during hunting season, so you can drive to the next milepoint. Gentle grades.

1.3   Pass more old gate posts, then make a sharp left turn at a wide parking area to stay on the blazed trail. (Straight ahead, FR236 continues, unblazed, past a locked gate, for about 1.7 mi to an intersection with the Milford Gap Tr near the Hazard Mill campground. FR236 is an easy hike to the camp, even when grass and annual weeds are high in late summer.)

The blazed trail follows an old stagecoach route over the mountain. Unfortunately, the well-built stage road is now badly eroded.

1.7 Switchback right. This is a good example of a "turning circle," extended from the slope on rock fill, to provide a level area for the coach and horses to make the sharp turn.

1.8 Milford Gap Tr, white-blazed. [1340] Straight ahead, the Milford Gap Tr ascends to the ridge in 0.6 mi. Right turn, it descends to the campground.

Kennedy Peak Circuit

Difficulty: Rise 1320 ft, steep.
Length: 9.2 mi.
Maps: PATC G (G-H, 19-21) and TI 792.
Approach: Edinburg - Luray.
Parking: See text.

The circuit has two vehicle access points, Edith Gap and a parking lot just east of Camp Roosevelt, both on SR675. The circuit can be hiked in either direction from either access point. This description provides a clockwise route to and from the lower access point near Camp Roosevelt. Park in the parking area on the Massanutten Tr.

Miles

0.0 The Stephens Tr, yellow-blazed, begins at the entrance to the parking area, [1280] where the Massanutten Tr turns sharp right off the entrance road near a storage shed. Follow yellow blazes out of the north end of the parking lot. The trail winds in and out of drains, along the base of the mountain, then begins to ascend.

3.8 Cross a wagon road and begin steep ascent on switchbacks.

4.7 T-junction with Massanutten Tr, orange-blazed. Turn right.

5.5 Junction with Kennedy Peak Tr, white-blazed, where Massanutten Tr bears right to skirt the peak. Bear left, following white blazes, on a rising ridge.

5.7 Kennedy Peak. [2600] Excellent views from wooden deck above stone shelter. Begin return by descending Kennedy Peak Tr.

6.0 Junction with Massanutten Tr, orange-blazed. Turn left.

6.1 Short, unblazed loop trail to right offers view to west.

6.8 Join old wagon road along the ridge, open to Off-Highway Vehicles.

8.4 Edith Gap, SR675. (Parking on both sides of road.) Turn right along road for 35 yds, then reenter woods on Massanutten Tr, orange-blazed. Steep descent. Pass large pit and trench mines on left, where iron ore was extracted for processing at Caroline Furnace in Fort Valley.

9.2 T-junction near storage shed, with yellow-blazed Stephens Tr on right. Turn right into parking area.

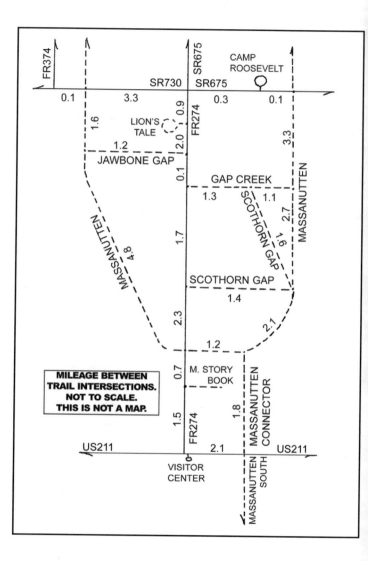

FR374

SR675

CAMP ROOSEVELT

SR730 SR675

0.1   3.3   0.3   0.1

1.6

LION'S TALE

0.9

FR274

2.0

1.2

JAWBONE GAP

0.1

GAP CREEK

1.3   1.1

SCOTHORN GAP

1.7

1.6

2.7

MASSANUTTEN

MASSANUTTEN

4.8

3.3

SCOTHORN GAP

1.4

2.3

2.1

1.2

M. STORY BOOK

0.7

MASSANUTTEN CONNECTOR

1.8

1.5

FR274

MASSANUTTEN SOUTH

US211

2.1

US211

VISITOR CENTER

MILEAGE BETWEEN TRAIL INTERSECTIONS. NOT TO SCALE. THIS IS NOT A MAP.

7. Crisman Hollow Group

THIS group of trails includes the area that is north of US211 and south of the intersection of SR675 and SR730. Crisman Hollow Rd, FR274, provides central access to most trails. There are two hollows and various ridges between Kerns Mountain on the west and Massanutten Mountain on the east. The headwaters of Passage Creek are in Crisman Hollow and Duncan Hollow. Camp Roosevelt is located just east of the junction of roads at the north end, and the Forest Service Visitor Center is on US211 diagonally across from the south end of FR274. The Lion's Tale and the Massanutten Story Book trails, located along FR274, are described in Chapter 10.

The mileage diagram illustrates the various circuit hikes that are possible using segments of the Massanutten Tr and the various side trails. Reliable water sources are available in Crisman and Duncan Hollows, and campsites are located along the trails. Duncan Knob (off the Gap Creek Tr) and Jawbone Overlook (off the Jawbone Gap Tr) offer opposing views across the hollow. A longer circuit to Bird Knob on the south half of Massanutten Mountain is possible using the Massanutten Connector Tr, Crisman Hollow Rd, and the trails in the South Group.

Timber rattlesnake on Crisman Hollow Rd
(by Wil Kohlbrenner)

Gap Creek Trail

Difficulty: Elevation change 850 ft, steep, loose tread, hidden hazards.

Length: 2.4 mi.   *Blazes:* Blue, dotted-i.
Maps: PATC G (F-G, 24) and TI 792.
Approach: Crisman Hollow Rd (FR274).
Parking: Along FR274 or along a loop driveway that connects hunter campsites on the east of the road (10).

This east-west trail rises into Peach Orchard Gap between Duncan Knob and Middle Mountain, then descends to the Massanutten Tr in Duncan Hollow. A side trip to Duncan Knob is possible for the adventurous hiker/climber. The trailhead on Crisman Hollow Rd is about 100 yds south of the trailhead for the Jawbone Gap Tr, also blazed blue.

East West

0.0 2.4 FR274. [1650] Eastbound, follow dirt road, turn left at first camping area.

0.1 2.3 Wooden bridge over reliable Passage Creek. Wide trail, switchbacks, steep, loose tread.

0.7 1.7 Wildlife pond, south.

1.3 1.1 Scothorn Gap Tr, yellow-blazed. [2300] Eastbound, turn left, continue ascent. Westbound, bear right, descend.

Steep.

1.5 0.9 Peach Orchard Gap. [2500] Broad, flat area. Large campsite. A short spur trail, white-blazed, leads north to the base of Duncan Knob. A large stack of rocks marks the end of the white-blazed trail. Small rock piles mark a possible route to the top of the knob [2800]. (After descending from the knob, be sure to locate the white-blazed spur trail for return.) Descend, east or west.

Steep, rocky switchbacks. Sections of collapsing tread. Sections of tread are a deep V shape, with hidden rocks under leaves or snow. Poor footing. Occasionally muddy.

2.4 0.0 Massanutten Tr (north CCW 42.8, south CW 28.3), orange-blazed. [1870] Large campsite to the east just across the reliable creek. Westbound, ascend on a wide roadbed at first.

Jawbone Gap Trail

Difficulty: Elevation change 750 ft, steep.
Length: 1.2 mi.   *Blazes:* Blue, dotted-i.
Maps: PATC G (F, 24) and TI 792.
Approach: Crisman Hollow Rd (FR274).
Parking: Along FR274 (6). (Do not block gate at trailhead.)

This east-west trail ascends to Jawbone Gap on Kerns Mountain. In 1980, this entire area was burned in a 10,000-acre forest fire. The area was logged to recover damaged timber, and the trail was lost. In 1997, the trail was reopened, partly on logging roads.

Be alert to possible changes in this trail if a shelter is constructed on the logging road section.

West   East

0.0   1.2   Crisman Hollow Rd, FR274. [1650] Westbound, ascend on gated forest road, known as Turkey Pen Rd.

0.2   1.0   Wildlife clearing, north. Rock outcrops on far side hang over Passage Creek. The high end of the clearing is a helicopter drop point during fire fighting.

0.3   0.9   T-junction. (Unblazed road goes north for 1.5 mi.) Westbound, turn left and pass an unblazed trail to left that descends to a wildlife pond. Eastbound, turn right, descend.

0.4   0.8   Spring, unreliable, that feeds the pond through a culvert under the road.

0.5   0.7   Westbound, bear right at a fork, onto grassy logging road. (The unblazed left fork, known as Old Turkey Pen Rd, descends for 0.3 mi to Crisman Hollow Rd. It meets the road about 0.3 mi south of the trailhead.)

Switchbacks on wide, grassy logging road.

0.8   0.4   Westbound, turn sharp right off logging road onto narrow woods trail. Eastbound, turn left onto wide grassy road.

Steep, narrow tread. Switchbacks. Occasional views of Duncan Knob across Crisman Hollow.

1.2   0.0   Jawbone Gap. [2400] Massanutten Tr (south CCW 32.0, north CW 39.1), orange-blazed. A white-blazed spur trail climbs north 200 yards [+120] to Jawbone Overlook. Excellent views east and west. Fire-scarred stumps can be seen on this rewarding climb to the knob. Eastbound, descend on narrow woods trail.

Massanutten Connector Trail

Difficulty: Elevation change 370 ft, steep, loose tread.
Length: 1.8 mi.   *Blazes:* White, dotted-i.
Maps: PATC G (G-H, 28) and TI 792.
Approach: Luray – New Market.
Parking: Parking (40), south of US211.

This north-south trail connects the Massanutten Tr, on the north half of Massanutten, to US211 and to the trailhead of the Massanutten South Tr.

North   South

0.0   1.8   US211. [1130] Northbound, pass a gate and hike up FR415 between steep, cut banks.

Trail follows forest road, gentle grades.

1.1   0.7   Northbound, turn left off forest road onto narrower logging road, brushy. (If you miss this turn, you will find yourself at a turn-around area at the end of the forest road.) Southbound, turn right onto forest road.

Pass through a wildlife clearing with a good view of Strickler Knob to the east.

1.6   0.2   Northbound, begin narrow woods path, brushy. Southbound, join old logging road, grassy.

Two short switchbacks on a steep cross slope.

1.8   0.0   Massanutten Tr (east CCW 38.0, west CW 33.1), orange-blazed. [1500] Bear right for points on the east ridges of the Massanutten, turn left for points on the west ridges. Southbound, ascend on narrow sidehill tread.

Scothorn Gap Trail

Difficulty:	Elevation change 600 ft, steep, loose tread.
Length:	3.0 miles. *Blazes:* Yellow, dotted-i.
Maps:	PATC G (F-G, 24-26) and TI 792.
Approach:	Crisman Hollow Rd (FR274).
Parking:	Along FR274 (2) or along the trail itself (4).

This east-west trail climbs to a saddle between Middle and Waterfall mountains where it touches the Massanutten Tr, then turns north in the drainage between the mountains, and ends at the Gap Creek Tr.

Passage Creek at Scothorn Trail crossing (by Wil Kohlbrenner)

East   West

0.0   3.0   FR274. [1900] Eastbound, descend towards Passage Creek.

0.1   2.9   Cross Passage Creek, reliable; ascend.

This old logging road is occasionally wet, often steep, with deep waterbars. In places, the tread is loose and the footing is poor when wet or covered with leaves or snow.

1.1   1.9   Wildlife clearings, mowed every few years to keep them from reverting to forest. Campsites in the clearings and tentsites under trees. Westbound, begin descent.

1.2   1.8   Eastbound, leave the road on a narrower trail to the right. (The road bears left to another wildlife clearing.) Reenter woods, with a pond on the left. Beavers extended this pond downstream and put an earlier version of this trail under water, which caused the Forest Service to relocate the trail around the high side of the pond. Beavers were then driven out by two years of extreme drought, and perhaps a diminishing food supply.

1.3 **1.7** Unreliable spring on a short unblazed path north of the trail.

1.4 **1.6** Massanutten Tr (easterly CCW 40.1, southerly CW 30.0), orange-blazed. [2500] Eastbound, turn left to remain on Scothorn Gap Tr. Westbound, turn right to remain on Scothorn Gap Tr.

1.6 **1.4** Old section of the trail, west. Beaver ponds have dried up and this older section of the trail may be passable, but is likely marshy.

Gentle grades on old wagon road. Pass along east edge of wildlife clearings. In wooded areas, the tread may be wet from seeps.

2.3 **0.7** A small knoll on the far side of a clearing offers a limited view into Crisman Hollow. This is probably an old farm site.

3.0 **0.0** Gap Creek Tr, blue-blazed. [2300] Westbound, head south on a wide wagon road, gentle ascent.

Fawn hunkered down in the grass (by Wil Kohlbrenner)

8. South Group

SOUTH of US211, Massanutten Mountain is comprised of two to four parallel ridges, trending northeast to southwest. Most of the inner valleys flow eastward through water gaps into the South Fork of the Shenandoah. One stream, Mountain Run, flows westward into the North Fork of the Shenandoah.

Road access points are at the north end from US211, along the east from FR65, called Cub Run Rd, and from one point on the west at Fridley Gap. The southern tip of the mountain is privately owned.

The Forest Service operates the Massanutten Visitor Center on US211 in New Market Gap. When it is open, free Forest Service brochures are available, maps and books may be purchased, and the volunteer staff can answer questions.

The Wildflower Tr connects the Massanutten Visitor Center to the Massanutten South Tr. The Wildflower and Discovery Way trails are described in Chapter 10.

Massanutten South Trail

Difficulty: Cumulative elevation change about 4300 ft. Steep, loose tread.

Length: 19.6 mi.   *Blazes:* Orange, dotted-i.

Maps: PATC H (D-G, 1-15) and TI 792.

Approach: Luray – New Market; Cub Run Rd; Big Mountain Rd.

Parking: Parking lot (40) off US211. Also (many) along FR375, Big Mountain Rd, from Pitt Spring north to the TV tower access road. Also (6) along southern end of FR65, Cub Run Rd.

The trail starts from a parking lot on the south edge of US211 two miles east of the Massanutten Visitor Center at New Market Gap. This trailhead is directly across US211 from the Massanutten Connector Tr, white-blazed.

From the parking lot, the trail ascends westward, joining the Wildflower Tr for a short section then climbs to an overlook on the westernmost ridge of the mountain. It passes the Bird Knob

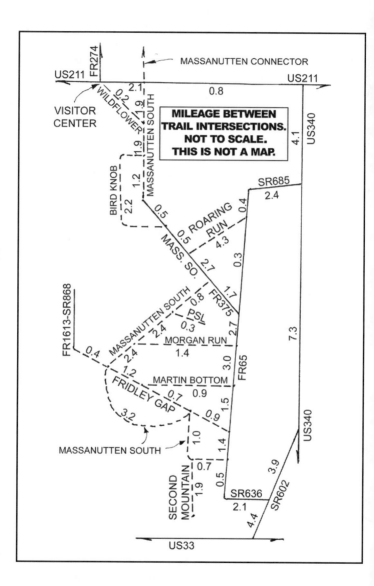

MASSANUTTEN CONNECTOR

US211 · FR274

US211

VISITOR CENTER

WILDFLOWER

2.1
0.2
1.9

0.8

MILEAGE BETWEEN TRAIL INTERSECTIONS. NOT TO SCALE. THIS IS NOT A MAP.

MASSANUTTEN SOUTH

1.9

4.1

US340

BIRD KNOB

1.2

2.2

0.5

SR685

2.4

ROARING RUN

0.4

0.5

MASS. SO.

4.3

2.7

0.3

1.7

FR1613-SR868

FR375

0.8

2.7

PSL

MASSANUTTEN SOUTH

0.4

2.4

0.3

2.4

MORGAN RUN

1.4

7.3

1.2

3.0

FR65

MARTIN BOTTOM

FRIDLEY GAP

0.7

0.9

MASSANUTTEN SOUTH

3.2

0.9

1.5

1.0

1.4

US340

SECOND MOUNTAIN

0.7

0.5

3.9

1.9

SR636

SR602

2.1

4.4

US33

Tr, then continues southward to a junction with FR375, Big Mountain Rd, and descends along the road into the drainage area that is west of Big Mountain.

At Pitt Spring, the trail leaves the descending road and climbs in the drainage area west of Third Mountain, passing the Pitt Spring Lookout Tr, to an intersection with the Morgan Run Tr. It continues south, rising and falling in the valley between Third and Fourth mountains to an intersection with the Fridley Gap Tr. The trail then ascends toward Grubbs Knob on Fourth Mountain. Before reaching the knob, it turns east and descends, crossing Fridley Run, and climbing again to cross Third Mountain, and drop into the saddle between Second and Third mountains, where it again meets the Fridley Gap Tr. It then turns south along Boone Run, past the Boone Run Shelter, and turns east through Runkles Gap and onto FR65, Cub Run Rd.

Many sections of the trail are maintained as a wide fire access road.

Historical note: South of Pitt Spring, for about a mile, the trail is in an area of old wagon roads and mines. Mine entrances (adits) are collapsed and sealed, but the depressed areas are evident in the steep slope. Near each adit is a mine dump, a flat-topped mound of dirt on an otherwise steep slope. The mines supplied iron ore to Catherine Furnace.

South   North

0.0   19.6   US211. [1130] Southbound, descend. Ignore red "blazes" that mark the forest boundary.

On old roads, cross several small streams.

0.4   19.2   Cross powerline right-of-way.

1.6   18.0   Southbound, turn right on logging road then right again in 100 yds onto forest road. Northbound, be alert to these left turns off forest road and logging road.

1.7   17.9   Locked gate where forest road meets a loop road for a former picnic area. Southbound, bear left on loop road; in 120 yds, turn left to join Wildflower Tr, white-blazed. Northbound, bear right onto loop road, in 120 yds, bear right again onto gated forest road.

1.9   **17.7**   Southbound, turn left off Wildflower Tr [1700], and begin steep ascent [+1040] at north end of Massanutten Mountain. Northbound, merge right with Wildflower Tr, white-blazed, descend.

2.3   **17.3**   Ridge. [2040] Red paint marks a National Forest corner.

       Very steep tread follows the rocky ridge on the north end of the mountain.

3.0   **16.6**   [2740] Panoramic views of the valley of the North Fork of the Shenandoah, with New Market in the middle distance, Great North Mountain along the West Virginia border on the horizon.

       Level hiking on narrow woods path along ridge.

3.8   **15.8**   Bird Knob Tr, white-blazed, west. [2780] Southbound, bear left and continue for 30 yds to clearing.

       Almost level, 20-ft wide grassy/sandy road.

4.1   **15.5**   Road west leads to Bird Knob Tr in 85 yds.

4.2   **15.4**   Road west leads to Bird Knob Tr in 35 yds.

4.7   **14.9**   Road west [2800] leads to wildlife clearing and pond in 100 yds.

5.0   **14.6**   Locked gate, at a sharp turn in FR375, Big Mountain Rd. [2740] (FR375 ascends past a locked gate to a TV tower on Big Mountain [2960], but trees obscure views.)

       Southbound, follow FR375, descending.

5.5   **14.1**   Bird Knob Tr, white-blazed, west. [2520]

6.0   **13.6**   Roaring Run Tr, purple-blazed, east. [2400]

6.8   **12.8**   Gas pipeline right-of-way crosses.

7.8   **11.8**   Power line right-of-way crosses.

8.7   **10.9**   Pitt Spring. [1750] Southbound, trail goes west off road, crossing Pitt Spring Run on a wooden bridge. Parking (10) at a turn in road. Camping area on mine dump west of the run. Adits nearby. Steep tread, kept open as a fire access road.

8.8   **10.8**   Old wagon road, west, overgrown, descends at a shallow angle to adits and mine dumps on downslope.

9.0   **10.6**   Mine dumps and adits, east, on upslope.

9.4   **10.2**   Rock cairn, west, marks unblazed trail which leads to west ridge with limited views to west.

9.5   **10.1**   Pitt Spring Lookout Tr, white-blazed, east. [2200]

9.7   **9.9**   Midpoint of a U-shaped wildlife clearing to east. No campsites.

9.9   **9.7**   Large, multi-tent campsite 100 yds to east on a road that leaves at a shallow angle. Wildlife pond. [2150]

10.5   **9.1**   Wildlife pond east, below trail.

11.6   **8.0**   Unblazed trail, west, leads to private property.

12.0   **7.6**   Morgan Run crosses trail, flowing west to east. Morgan Run Tr, yellow-blazed, goes east about 35 yds south of the run. [2180] Southbound, begin ascent on tread that is often wet from seeps.

12.5   **7.1**   Morgan Run crosses trail, flowing east to west.

13.0   **6.6**   Southbound, begin loose tread, often wet. Northbound, tread is firmer.

13.2   **6.4**   Saddle between Third and Fourth mountains. [2490] About 65 yds of solid tread! Southbound, descend along Mountain Run on loose tread. Northbound, descend along Morgan Run on loose tread.

13.4   **6.2**   Southbound, start smooth, grassy tread, deep dips to control runoff. Northbound, start loose tread.

13.5   **6.1**   South end of fire access road. Old road leaves, west, at a shallow angle. Southbound, begin descent along stream. Northbound, begin steep ascent on wide, grassy tread.

Trail is in stream bed, frequent crossings. Trail serves as alternate stream bed in flood conditions.

14.3   **5.3**   Fridley Gap Tr, purple-blazed, joins from east. [1900] Wooden walkway just north of this point.

Fridley Gap Tr runs concurrent with Massanutten South Tr, orange and purple blazes. Steep, loose tread.

14.4   **5.2**   Fridley Gap Tr, purple-blazed, joins from west. [1820] Southbound, cross Fridley Run and ascend toward Grubbs Knob. Campsites here.

Occasional views to west from cliffs.

16.0   **3.6**   Reverse direction in a sweeping turn at high point below Grubbs Knob. [2900] Descend, each direction.

16.5   **3.1**   Cross Fridley Run. Ascend, each direction. Pile of limestone dust nearby for liming the run.

17.2   **2.4**   Third Mountain ridge. [2800] Descend, each direction.

17.6   **2.0**   Fridley Gap Tr, purple-blazed. [2610] Southbound, turn right, descend. Northbound, turn left, ascend.

18.6   **1.0**   Shelter Tr, white-blazed, goes south 100 yds to Boone Run Shelter. [1900] (Shelter is three-sided, has a privy, and an unreliable spring beyond.) Southbound, descend, cross Boone Run, reliable.

18.7   **0.9**   Second Mountain Tr, blue-blazed, south. [1880]

Four crossings of Boone Run. Rocky tread where floods have used the trail as a stream bed.

19.4   **0.2**   FR65. Cub Run Rd near Runkles Gap. [1590]

19.6   **0.0**   Gate on FR65, Cub Run Rd (usually open). Small parking lot nearby, but entry ramp is eroded.

Bird Knob Trail

Difficulty: Elevation change 330 ft.
Length: 2.2 mi.   *Blazes:* White, dotted-i.
Maps: PATC H (D, 3-4) and TI 792.
Approach: Big Mountain Rd, FR375.
Parking: Along Big Mountain Rd (4).

This north-south trail forms a loop to the west of the Massanutten South Tr. It crosses the drainage system west of Big Mountain to a clearing at the foot of Bird Knob, then turns north along the ridge of Massanutten Mountain.

The Lord Fairfax Line (the southwest boundary of Lord Fairfax's domain) crosses the Massanutten just at the foot and on the north of Bird Knob. All of the Northern Neck had natural boundaries except the southwest, which is a straight line 76 miles long. The line was surveyed in 1746 by Thomas Lewis, a friend of George Washington, and by Peter Jefferson, father of Thomas Jefferson. A reprint of Thomas Lewis' journal, recorded daily during the survey, is available for purchase at the Massanutten Visitor Center.

North   South

0.0   2.2   Massanutten South Tr, orange-blazed, on FR375. [2520] Northbound, descend on a gated logging road.

0.1   2.1   A woods road, north, leads upslope for 200 yds to a pretty wildlife pond and large campsite beyond.

0.2   2.0   Cross drainage below pond, ascend.

0.4   1.8   Wildlife clearing at foot of Bird Knob. [2570] This is the corner of Page, Rockingham, and Shenandoah counties. Small pond on the far side of the clearing. Bird Knob, south of the clearing, is thickly wooded with regrowth, has no trail, and offers little in views. Skirt the north of the clearing. Northbound, turn right on woods path. Southbound, turn east, join a logging road, descending.

Trail follows ridge line, high point [2850], with the valley of the North Fork of the Shenandoah to the west. Trees obscure the view, but the murmur of commerce in the valley offers an interesting contrast to the silence from the east.

1.8   0.4   Road crosses. A block field on the slope of the mountain, 200 yds to the west, offers a limited winter view. The road east leads to Massanutten South Tr in 35 yds.

1.9   0.3   Road east leads to Massanutten South Tr in 85 yds.

2.2   0.0   Massanutten South Tr, orange-blazed. [2780] Southbound, trail follows the ridge.

Fridley Gap Trail

Difficulty: Elevation change 1200 ft, steep, loose tread.
Length: 3.2 mi. *Blazes:* Purple, dotted-i.
Maps: PATC H (E-G, 13) and TI 792.
Approach: East end: Cub Run Rd (FR65). West end: see below.
Parking: East end (6): along Cub Run Rd. West end: see below.

This east-west trail crosses the southern half of the Massanutten, south of its mid-point. The trail climbs from the west through Fridley Gap, a water gap between Massanutten Mountain and Fourth Mountain. It crosses the Massanutten South Tr, crosses Third Mountain to the Martin Bottom Tr, turns south and ascends along Cub Run to again intersect the Massanutten South Tr, then turns east to cross Second Mountain and descend to Cub Run Rd.

To approach the west trailhead from I-81, take exit 257 and follow US11 south through the community of Lacey Spring. (If coming north on I-81, take exit 251 and follow US11 north toward Lacey Spring.) South of the Lacey Spring post office, turn east on SR806, Martz Rd, then right at a T-junction onto SR620, Mountain Valley Rd. Follow SR620 for 1.7 mi and turn left onto SR722, Armentrout Path. After 0.3 mi on SR722, turn left onto SR868, Airey Lane. At end of state maintenance, continue onto FR1613, a public access right-of-way. At 1.1 mi from SR722, the road makes a sharp turn left, uphill. Parking areas (8) near this turn. Do not block the road.

East   West

0.0   3.2   Parking on FR1613. [1660] Eastbound, hike east from turn in road.

Mountain Run is in a hollow, south. Tread is on large rocks, steep for 130 yds.

0.2   3.0   Eastbound, turn right on a wagon road. Westbound, turn left off road.

Wagon road threads through Fridley Gap, a narrow gap with steep walls of broken rock. Hemlock and hardwood forest provides good canopy. In places the road is just a rocky wash left behind when floods overflowed into roadbed.

0.35 2.85 Large, popular pool for wading, south. Cross the left fork of two creeks that join here to form Mountain Run.

0.4 2.8 Massanutten South Tr, orange-blazed. [1820] (Campsites to south along Massanutten South Tr.) Eastbound, turn north. Westbound, turn west, cross creek.

Orange and purple blazes, steep, loose tread.

0.5 2.7 Massanutten South Tr, orange-blazed. [1900] Westbound, turn south. Eastbound, turn east, ascend [+800].

Extremely steep, rocky tread, often gutted, with many loose rocks of all sizes in tread. When covered with fallen leaves or snow, the footing is treacherous. NOTE: This section of the trail may have been relocated onto switchbacks.

1.0 2.2 Views develop to west, south, and east from rocks.

1.3 1.9 Top of Third Mountain. [2700] Trail follows the ridge for a few yds, then descends steeply in both directions.

1.6 1.6 Martin Bottom Tr, blue-blazed. [2400] Eastbound, turn right. Westbound, bear left, ascend, steep.

Trail is on a wide fire-access road, with unreliable Cub Run to the east.

2.3 0.9 Massanutten South Tr, on a saddle between Second and Third Mountains, where both trails make right-angle turns. [2610] Eastbound, gradual ascent of Second Mountain. Westbound, turn north; gradual descent.

2.6 0.6 Ridge of Second Mountain. [2650] Descend. Tread is narrow and steep.

3.2 0.0 Cub Run Rd. [2150] Westbound, ascend.

Martin Bottom Trail

Difficulty: Elevation change 360 ft, loose and muddy tread.
Length: 0.9 mi.   *Blazes:* Blue, dotted-i.
Maps: PATC H (F-G, 12) and TI 792.
Approach: Cub Run Rd (FR65).

Parking: Along Cub Run Rd (5).

This short east-west trail follows a gated forest road from Cub Run Rd up Martin Bottom to a junction with the Fridley Gap Tr. The trail parallels the upper portion of Cub Run, crossing the run twice. The trail is kept open as a fire access road.

West   East

0.0   0.9   Cub Run Rd. [2040] Westbound, follow road. Pass locked gate.

Loose tread on crushed stone surface.

0.4   0.5   Two crossings of Cub Run at dips in road. Crushed stone surface ends at turnaround area between the crossings.

Grassy logging road. Muddy sections, due to seeps, may be filled with crushed stone.

0.5   0.4   Unreliable spring, north.

0.9   0.0   Fridley Gap Tr, purple-blazed. [2400] East-bound, follow grassy roadbed.

Morgan Run Trail

Difficulty: Elevation change 580 ft, steep, scrambles, slippery rock tread, very wet. (Photo on page 121)

Length: 1.4 mi.   *Blazes:* Yellow, dotted-i.

Maps: PATC H (E-F, 10) and TI 792.

Approach: Cub Run Rd (FR65).

Parking: Along Cub Run Rd (6).

This east-west trail ascends along Morgan Run, through a narrow, rocky hemlock gorge, to intersect the Massanutten South Tr. The narrow tread follows an old wagon road, occasionally supported by rock retaining walls above the bed of the run. Much of the tread in the gorge is on rocks that are covered with green-black algae and various club mosses. These are slippery even when dry. There are five crossings of the run, and a long section in the bed of the run. After heavy rains, the trail may be impassable. Most hikers either love this trail or hate it. Pay attention to blazes when negotiating rocks in the run.

West	East	
0.0	**1.4**	Cub Run Rd. [1600] Westbound, leave the road

0.0   **1.4**   Cub Run Rd. [1600] Westbound, leave the road on a tank-trapped wagon road, which is north of the culvert that takes the reliable run under the road. Steep ascent along bank, well above Morgan Run. In 100 ft, a wildlife clearing on right that is overrun with autumn olive.

0.1   **1.3**   Cozy two-tent campsite, south, below tread.

0.2   **1.2**   Westbound, descend into gorge, tread is on rocks.

Steep rock slopes, left and right. Cross and recross the run. Frequent steep tread. Tread is often gutted, and serves as an alternate stream bed when water is high. "Caves" under rock overhangs, north.

0.4   **1.0**   Tread, above run, is collapsing into the gorge.

0.5   **0.9**   Flat table rock in tread.

Big opening under rock outcrop, north. Interesting patterns on underside of rock overhang.

0.6   **0.8**   Tread follows the middle of the run.

0.7   **0.7**   Top of hemlock gorge. Westbound, begin narrow, brushy trail under mixed hemlock and hardwoods. Eastbound, begin steep, rocky tread in gorge.

Wading pools in stream, north. Muddy tread.

1.2   **0.2**   Right-angle turn in trail. Unblazed trail, south, leads to campsite.

1.4   **0.0**   Massanutten South Tr, orange-blazed. [2180] Eastbound, gentle descent.

Pitt Spring Lookout Trail

Difficulty: Rise 200 ft, steep.
Length: 0.3 mi.   *Blazes:*   White, dotted-i.
Maps: PATC H (E, 8) and TI 792.
Approach: From Massanutten South Tr.

This spur trail ascends eastward from the Massanutten South Tr to the foundation of a former fire lookout tower, where there is a narrow view to the east across the valley of the South Fork of the Shenandoah and on to the Blue Ridge.

East

0.0   Massanutten South Tr. [2200] Ascend; often steep.

0.2   Fork in trail. Unblazed, poorly maintained trail to the right circles below the tower site and along another ridge for about 0.4 mi, with occasional winter views. No campsites on this side trail.

0.3   Campsite under pines on overlook. [2400] Foundation of old firetower nearby.

Roaring Run Trail

Difficulty: Rise 450 ft eastbound, 1750 ft westbound, steep.

Length: 4.3 mi.   *Blazes:* Purple, dotted-i.

Maps: PATC H (D-F, 4-7) and TI 792.

Approach: East end: Cub Run Rd. West End: Big Mountain Rd.

Parking: East end: Near Catherine Furnace (6). West end: along Big Mountain Rd (5).

This east-west trail begins near Catherine Furnace, and connects Cub Run Rd, FR65, to the Massanutten South Tr on FR375. The trail ascends on a wagon road along Roaring Run for one mile, crosses a service road for a pipeline, and continues along a feeder stream, then a flat area, then crosses the ridge of Big Mountain and descends to an intersection with the Massanutten South Tr, on Big Mountain Rd (FR375).

West   East

0.0   4.3   Cub Run Rd. [1100] Westbound, ascend on wagon road, closed to vehicles by rock slabs. Just west of the rocks, note the black charcoal dust on the ground. This edge of the trail supported a bridge to the top of the furnace. Iron ore, limestone and charcoal were trundled across the bridge and dumped into the furnace. The tread has small black stones – crushed slag that was used to surface the roadbed. The area west of this point passes through the furnace community. More recent foundations are from a CCC camp that reused this area in the 1930s.

0.2	**4.1**	Cross Roaring Run.
0.5	**3.8**	Wagon road is high on a steep bank above

Roaring Run.

1.0   **3.3**   Westbound, cross a feeder stream and turn left. (Straight ahead for 30 yds to reach main stream and the gas pipeline's right-of-way.) Begin ascent along feeder stream. Forks in old road. Pay attention to blazes.

1.3   **3.0**   Cross forest road. (North, road crosses the pipeline, and drops to Roaring Run in 1.1 miles. South, road T's into Big Mountain Rd in 1.3 miles.)

Steep grassy road bed.

2.1   **2.2**   Cross pipeline. (Pipeline climbs steeply over ridge of Big Mountain.) Westbound, end of road. Eastbound, join road.

2.8   **1.5**   Sag known as Roaring Run Gap. [2350]

Steep switchbacks, brushy in summer.

3.4   **0.9**   Ridge of Big Mountain. [2850] Descend.

Steep, switchbacked.

4.3   **0.0**   Massanutten South Tr, orange-blazed, on Big Mountain Rd. [2400] Eastbound, ascend.

Second Mountain Trail

Difficulty: Rise 1080 ft (to knob), steep.
Length: 1.9 mi.   *Blazes:* Blue, dotted-i.
Maps: PATC H (F, 15-16) and TI 792.
Approach: From Massanutten South Tr.

This north-south trail provides an interesting hike to Kaylor Knob. Good blueberry picking in July! Many rodents and nesting birds – and the poisonous and non-poisonous snakes that prey on them.

South

0.0   Massanutten South Tr. [1880] Follow blue blazes across Boone Run and ascend.

Six switchbacks before attaining the ridge. Note the excellent stone retaining wall under this sidehill trail, no doubt the work of the Civilian Conservation Corps, as well as the many milemarkers along the trail.

0.4   Attain the ridge line, ascend along the ridge, with views east across the South Fork of the Shenandoah to the Blue Ridge.

1.7   Fork. Sitting rock. Forest Service blazes may end here. *Take left fork.* (Other blazing may have been done by Massanutten Resort folks that use these trails. The right fork leads to private property.)

1.9   Kaylor Knob. [2960] Views east and south towards Elkton. (A well-worn trail continues south past the knob, initially descending, then following a long sharp ridge to private property.) Return from the knob to the fork, then bear right on officially blazed trail, or see separate description, Kaylor Knob Bushwhack, below.

Grubbs Knob Circuit

Difficulty: Cumulative rise (and fall) 1800 ft, steep, loose and muddy tread, stream crossings. Compass recommended for optional climb of knob.

Length: 6.9 mi, basic circuit,
            7.7 mi, circuit with optional climb of knob.

Maps: PATC H (E-G, 12-14) and TI 792.

Approach: Cub Run Rd (FR 65).

Parking: Along Cub Run Rd (6).

This hike uses the Martin Bottom Tr (0.9 mi) to access a 5.1 mi circuit on the Fridley Gap and Massanutten South trails. An optional bushwhack to the top of Grubbs Knob [3100] can be done along the way.

Miles

0.0   Cub Run Rd at Martin Bottom Tr. [2040] Hike west on Martin Bottom Tr, blue-blazed. Gradual ascent on gravel road, then on grassy road.

0.9   Fridley Gap Tr, purple-blazed. Begin a clockwise route by walking straight ahead, purple blazes. Gentle ascent with Cub Run in a ravine, left.

1.6 Massanutten South Tr, orange-blazed. Turn right, ascend Third Mountain, following orange blazes.

2.0 Bear left around north ridge of Third Mountain and descend into hollow between Third and Fourth mountains.

2.8 Bear right, cross Fridley Run, ascend.

3.2 Switchback, continue steep ascent toward Grubbs Knob.

3.5 Where the trail bears right in a flat area, away from knob, watch for an unblazed trail left. This trail leads to the knob in 0.4 mi. [+300] (Limited view.) The trail is faint and easy to lose coming down, so take compass headings going up in order to plan the route down. On return to the blazed trail, turn left to continue clockwise loop, descending. Good views west from cliffs on left of the trail.

5.0 Fridley Gap Tr, purple-blazed, joins from left, after crossing Fridley Run. Continue straight ahead, ascending, steep, loose tread, orange and purple blazes.

5.1 Turn right with Fridley Gap Tr, leaving Massanutten South Tr. Ascend Third Mountain [+800] on steep, rocky, gutted tread. Views develop (behind you) near the ridge.

5.7 Ridge of Third Mountain. [2700] Begin steep descent.

6.0 Martin Bottom Tr, blue-blazed, left. Turn left.

6.9 Cub Run Rd.

Kaylor Knob Bushwhack

Difficulty: Rise 1340 ft, steep, stream crossings, bushwhack return. Map and compass recommended. Handclippers useful for briars.

Length: ~ 5.5 mi.

Maps: PATC H (F-G, 15-16) and TI 792.

Approach: Cub Run Rd (FR 65), near Runkles Gap.

Parking: Along Cub Run Rd (6), where orange-blazed.

The route to Kaylor Knob follows Second Mountain Tr. The return route is a bushwhack into the valley between Second Mountain and First Mountain, followed by a bushwhack along an old wagon road that criss-crosses the drainage system between the mountains. Various events (foot races, bicycle races) are run on these trails from the private property at the south end of the mountain. Trails described here as "unblazed" may have non-standard blazes applied by the sponsors of the events.

Miles

0.0   From edge of Cub Run Rd, follow orange-blazed Massanutten South Tr, crossing Boone Run four times. Watch for a blue alert blaze just before the fifth crossing of the run. Turn left on Second Mountain Tr, blue-blazed.

0.7   Cross Boone Run and climb steep bank on first of six switchbacks before attaining the ridge. Continue ascent along the ridge.

2.4   Fork in trail. Take left fork. Blazing may be confusing.

2.6   Kaylor Knob. [2960] Views east and south towards Elkton. Locate Hartman Knob on First Mountain – on a southeast heading. Your return route is in the valley between Kaylor and Hartman Knobs. To descend into the valley, first continue south from Kaylor Knob on a well-worn trail along the narrow crest of Second Mountain, descending for about a half mile. Sight back toward Hartman Knob until it is roughly east-northeast. Leave the ridge trail at any convenient location and begin an angling descent on the steep slope, along a northeast heading. This will bring you into a flat saddle between Kaylor Knob and Hartman Knob.

3.5   Saddle. Find an old wagon road and turn left on it, compass heading is roughly northeast. Follow the wagon road or stream bed as it descends in the drainage area. Eventually, the wagon road remains on higher ground, north and west of the stream. Stay on the wagon road, heading almost north towards Boone Run.

5.3   Wagon road bends right as it nears Boone Run. Stay on wagon road.

5.4   Cross Boone Run, follow wagon road up far side to Massanutten South Tr, orange-blazed. [1620] Turn right.

5.5   Cub Run Rd.

9. History

PEOPLE have lived on this land for about twelve millennia. They lived in the valleys, hunting and gathering. The valleys had areas of tall-grass prairie. Buffalo, as well as elk and deer were plentiful. Hunters used stone-tipped spears, but over the centuries new technologies arrived from the south and west: first the spear thrower, later the bow and arrow. Basket weaving, pottery making, and corn also arrived along trade routes. Eventually, corn, beans and squash were under cultivation, creating a more stable, year-round food supply that enabled larger communities to develop. The mountains were covered with climax forest. With only flaked stone tools and primitive agricultural methods, these people did not alter the land.

British colonists arrived in the 1600s, bringing grains (wheat, oats, rice, cool weather grasses), all types of livestock, wheeled conveyances, guns, iron tools, and Black African slaves. The valleys were cleared and planted. Tall-grass prairie was plowed under and planted with cool weather grasses that were more hardy to intensive grazing and cutting. Mountains were mined for iron ore. Forests were leveled for lumber, fuel, tanbark, and charcoal. In only 300 years the land was transformed.

All the Virginia buffalo, elk, deer, and their predators, the wolves and mountain lions, were killed. Deer were even hunted commercially, year-round, for their hides, like the great buffalo hunts in the late 1800s on the western plains. (Deer were restored in the early 1900s.) By 1900, the big trees were gone, mountains were eroding, streams were glutted with silt. Iron production had ceased, and iron furnace communities were disappearing.

The Forest Service was created in the early 1900s and began to purchase land under a "willing buyer, willing seller" policy. No one was forced to sell by government decree. This resulted in a jagged boundary for the national forest and left some privately held parcels, *inholdings*, surrounded entirely by national forest.

The Forest Service now manages most of the mountainous land, juggling the conflicting demands for timber, recreation, wilderness, wildlife, and clean water.

"Massanutten"

The origin of the Native American word "massanutten" is obscure. Two tales provide differing explanations. One tale states that wild sweet potatoes, called massanuttens, were planted by Native Americans in fields east of the mountain. Another tale states that the shape of Fort Valley reminded the Native Americans of their long woven baskets, called massanuttens.

Iron Making

Iron making was a major industry in the eastern United States in the 1800s and Virginia had its share of furnaces. In the Massanutten there were four. Two of these are on National Forest land: Elizabeth Furnace along Passage Creek at the north end of Fort Valley and Catherine Furnace along Cub Run on the east side of the southern half of Massanutten Mountain. Various features of iron furnace operation can be seen on the Pig Iron and Charcoal Trails at Elizabeth Furnace. The other furnaces are on private land and are not open to the public.

The furnaces were built in the early 1800s, and were declining by mid-century. They saw a brief revival as a source of iron for the Confederacy. Their extensive wooden structures were burned during the war, but some were rebuilt.

The iron that issued from a furnace and a nearby forge was transported in wagons to the South Fork of the Shenandoah, and from there in river barges to a railhead at Harpers Ferry on the Potomac. By the late 1800s, railroads into western Pennsylvania, coke from Pennsylvania coal, higher grade ore, and the loss of slave labor tipped the economics of iron making in favor of western Pennsylvania.

Iron Furnace Communities

This description may aid in visualizing the community that surrounded each iron furnace.

The furnace stack was always built close to the steep bank of a mountain stream. Dams and sluices brought a reliable flow of water to the base of the furnace to power a bellows. Large wooden structures were built on the bank above the furnace stack, with a bridge to the top of the furnace so that the furnace could be *charged* by dumping iron ore, limestone, and charcoal in from the top.

The furnace was set *into blast* by forcing air up through the charge. The furnace roared, cinders shot into the air. Intense heat and carbon monoxide from the burning charcoal stripped oxygen from iron oxides, leaving molten iron. Limestone, the *flux*, trapped free oxygen and other elements into a *slag* that floated on the molten iron.

When ready, the furnace was tapped. Molten iron ran out into a herringbone pattern in a flat bed of sand. The iron flowed along the pattern's spine, called the *sow*, and out into the ribs, the *pigs*. The slag was diverted to a separate area. The iron cooled and solidified. The pigs were broken from the sow and loaded onto wagons for transport to a downstream forge where water power was used again, to operate large hammers that pounded the brittle cast iron into wrought iron, transforming each pig into a *bloom*. Solidified slag was broken up and often used to surface roads.

As iron was hauled away from the furnace, more raw material arrived in heavy wagons from mines, hearths, and quarries. Wagon roads fanned out in all directions.

These labor intensive operations required fellers and colliers, miners and quarrymen, teamsters, wagonmakers, blacksmiths, sawyers, carpenters. Most of these workers lived near the furnace. Food for people and animals came from nearby farms and grist mills.

White families lived in tenant housing, single men in dormitories, black men and their families in slave quarters. There were barns and stables, as well as storage sheds for ore and charcoal. There was a one-room schoolhouse, a store with a post office, and one or more churches. The work was exhausting, alcoholism was rife, accidents frequent. Most furnace communities did not have a doctor. Midwives were kept busy, as childbearing and early infant death took its toll.

After the mid-1800s, furnaces began to go out of business. Men were idled, money disappeared, families moved away or fell back on an agricultural economy. The war between the states used up much of the manpower and draft animals. Slaves were freed. Some furnace stacks were taken down for building stones. The furnace stacks that remain are memorials to these once-thriving communities.

Hearths and Mines

Perhaps more interesting than the stone ruins of the furnaces are the hearths where charcoal was produced and the mines where iron ore was extracted. Today's blazed trails often follow old wagon roads in the forest. Hearths and mines appear along these old roads – if you know how to recognize them.

Hearths. A charcoal hearth is a level, circular area, about 15 paces in diameter. It is cut out of a gentle slope, so that one half has a cut bank, and the other half is raised (using dirt removed from the cut) to level the circle. It has a layer of charcoal dust under decayed leaves. A finger inserted into the leaves will come up jet black.

Hearths were generally near a spring or stream, since water was needed to control the charring process. A large pyramid of seasoned logs was built to form a kiln that contained the ten-day burning process. The *collier* lost everything if the slow burning of volatile vapors inside the kiln broke through the surface and reduced the wood to a pile of ashes. A small boy was often posted at a kiln, charged with the task of scurrying up a ladder leaning on the kiln to douse any breakthrough with water and patch the hole in the surface. When the color of the smoke indicated that charring was complete, openings around the base of the kiln were sealed to smother the fire. After a few days of cooling, the charcoal was carefully removed – with water handy to douse any remaining embers.

The collier built a series of hearths close to the source of logs and water, hauled logs to the hearths, then hauled away the charcoal – to be sold to the furnace owner at four cents a bushel. (Two hundred bushels were required to produce a ton of pig iron; a furnace in blast might produce two tons of iron per day.)

Faint wagon tracks that lead away from a main wagon road, often near a stream crossing, may lead to one or more hearths. These *coaling roads* are most easily seen in early spring, after winter rain and snow have plastered fallen leaves to the forest floor. A thin layer of snow on the ground further enhances the contours of the forest floor.

Each furnace required timber cutting rights to about 10,000 acres of forest land as a sustainable source of wood for charcoal making. Timber cutting for any purpose left *slash* behind. The mountains were burned repeatedly by wildfires that fed on this dead wood. Forest Service reports of the mountain land in the early 1900s tell of denuded, deeply eroded slopes, glutted streams, failing wells in the valleys. The Forest Service mandate came directly out of these reports: preserve watersheds and wisely manage the forest!

Mines. A mine can be an open trench, a pit, or a tunnel into the mountain. Mines are always served by an *ore road*.

A trench mine is a long ditch that followed a trace of ore chunks that were buried close to the surface. The chunks of ore probably broke loose from sedimentary rock layers and lay in stream beds during a time when the mountains were many times higher than today. These "ore beds" run uphill. Miners dug a trench to the required depth. Chunks of ore were carted down the trench to the ore road. Useless dirt was carted down the trench and dumped onto the slope. When the chunks of ore at the high end of the trench became scarce, a test pit was dug a few paces beyond, to see if the situation improved. Most trench mines end with one or two test pits.

Today, trench mines look like eroded stream beds, since they run uphill, but the trenches have no running water. Look for test pits at the high end and a fan-shaped dump area at the low end.

A pit mine was a deep, open pit alongside an exposed seam of rock at the base of a mountain slope. The ore was broken from the rock face. Overlying dirt that was removed to expose the seam, called the *overburden*, was dumped on the slope below the pit.

An underground mine had an entrance, called an *adit*. A *stulm*, or sloping shaft, was dug into the mountain, with supporting timbers to hold up the roof. A *drift*, or horizontal tunnel off the stulm, allowed the miners to work along a seam of ore. (Timbers have rotted away and all adits have been collapsed and sealed for safety reasons.)

The dump from any type of mine is a more-or-less level, fan-shaped area on a slope below the trench, pit, or adit.

Ore chunks from trench mines were very rough, and pitted. These required washing to remove clinging dirt. The washing took place in a sluice located near the mine. A small dam provided running water, and dirt washed from the ore produced a fan-shaped tailings dump. Tailings have probably been leveled by subsequent floods. Ore from pit mines and underground mines was solid rock and did not require washing.

Hearths and dumps are smooth, level areas that look like good campsites. A hearth is often near a spring or stream. However, camping on a hearth puts a layer of fine black dust on everything, including the camper!

Mile Markers. Carved stone slabs were erected every quarter mile along many trails by the Civilian Conservation Corps in the 1930s. They are about 16 inches high and irregular in shape. Some are missing, perhaps due to a relocation of the trail. The carved numbers are often hard to read due to weathering. Please do not try to enhance the numbers by scratching or writing on the stone! The next person who finds the stone will also enjoy deciphering the weathered carving.

The carved numbers look like a fraction, for example, 2/3. The digit above the slash indicates the mile, the digit below the slash indicates which quarter of that mile. Thus, 2/3 signifies the end of the third quarter of the second mile, or 1.75 miles from the trailhead. Two methods were used to mark the whole mile points. One method marks the end of a mile with a single digit. For example, the end of the first mile is recorded as a 1. The other method considers the end of the first mile to be the start of the second mile and records it as 2/0.

Mileage	Carved numbers
0	The trailhead is not marked.
0.25	**1/1**
0.50	**1/2**
0.75	**1/3**
1.0	**1** (or **2/0**)
1.25	**2/1**

1.5	**2/2**
1.75	**2/3**
2.0	**2** (or **3/0**)
2.25	**3/1**

If you find a marker, there may be another in a quarter mile. A tall hiker with a stride of 36 inches covers a quarter mile in 440 steps. Most hikers have a stride closer to 30 inches and require about 530 steps to go a quarter mile.

Stream crossing on Morgan Run Trail (by Wil Kohlbrenner)

10. Interpretive Trails

SIX trails on the Massanutten offer an introduction to the mountain, its attractions, and its history. The trails are short, easy hikes. Some are suitable for wheelchairs with assistance, one is universally accessible. These trails have signs and displays, but these are removed over the winter months for refurbishing and to reduce vandalism.

Charcoal Trail

Difficulty: Rise and fall, 100 ft.
Length: 0.6 mi.   *Blazes:* Unblazed.
Maps: PATC G (Eliz Furn inset) and TI 792.
Approach: Fort Valley Rd (SR 678).
Parking: Elizabeth Furnace Picnic Area (10).

This loop trail on the slope of Massanutten Mountain east of the picnic area offers displays and descriptive signs that explain the charcoal-making process that was essential to the operation of Elizabeth Furnace (and denuded most of the surrounding slopes). Follow signs from the east edge of the inner parking lot. The route is counter-clockwise.

Discovery Way Trail

Difficulty: Paved, suitable for wheelchairs.
Length: 0.2 mi.   *Blazes:* Unblazed.
Maps: PATC H (D, 1) and TI 792.
Approach: Luray – New Market.
Parking: At Massanutten Visitor Center on US 211 (15).

This shaded spur trail leaves from the far end of the parking lot. It offers explanations of items found along forest trails.

Lion's Tale Trail

Difficulty: Universally accessible.
Length: 0.4 mi.   *Blazes:* Unblazed.
Maps: PATC G (inset on back) and TI 792.
Approach: Crisman Hollow Rd (FR 274).
Parking: Parking lot (20) at trailhead, restrooms.

This interpretive trail was originally developed with funds from the Lions Clubs of Virginia, as a rope-guided trail for use by the sight-impaired. Signs in Braille (and in print) describe the forest through its textures, smells, and sounds. The trail is now universally accessible, including a ramp into the waters of Passage Creek. The trail has been included in the National Recreation Trails System.

Accessible pool on Lion's Tale Trail (by Wil Kohlbrenner)

Massanutten Story Book Trail

Difficulty: Paved, suitable for wheelchairs with assistance.
Length: 0.3 mi.   *Blazes:* Unblazed.
Maps: PATC G (G, 29) and TI 792.
Approach: Crisman Hollow Rd (FR 274).
Parking: Parking lot (10), along road.

This spur trail has signs along the trail that show the geological history of the mountain-making process. Panoramic view to the east from a platform at the end of the trail. Turkey beard in bloom in June among the rocks along the trail.

Pig Iron Trail

Difficulty: Cumulative rise and fall, 50 ft.
Length: 0.3 mi.   *Blazes:* Unblazed.
Maps: PATC G (Eliz Furn inset) and TI 792.
Approach: Fort Valley Rd (SR 678).
Parking: Elizabeth Furnace Picnic Area.

This loop trail circles the ruins of the Elizabeth Furnace, located along the Massanutten and Tuscarora trails just east of the picnic area. Signs explain the workings of a blast furnace. Best access to the trail is from the Charcoal Tr, although you can also approach along the Massanutten Tr.

Wildflower Trail

Difficulty: Fall 200 ft, steep.
Length: 0.5 mi.   *Blazes:* White, dotted-i.
Maps: PATC G (D, 29) and TI 792.
Approach: Luray – New Market.
Parking: Massanutten Visitor Center on US 211 (15).

This east-west trail descends from the Visitor Center to an abandoned picnic area, sharing some of its tread with the Massanutten South Trail. Signs explain the effect of people and creatures on forest health. The trail is noted for its display of wildflowers in season, especially pink ladyslippers in May. The trail tread is crushed stone.

East   West

0.0   0.5   Visitor Center. Eastbound, descend from left of the entrance drive.

0.3   0.2   Massanutten South Trail, orange-blazed, south, to all points south. Wildflower and Massanutten South trails share the tread, orange and white blazes.

0.5   0.0   Loop road for a former picnic area. Massanutten South Trail, orange-blazed, uses a section of the loop road. Westbound, ascend.